ECONOMIC DEVELOPMENT:
THE CULTURAL CONTEXT

ECONOMIC DEVELOPMENT

The Cultural Context

THOMAS R. DE GREGORI
Associate Professor of Economics
University of Houston

ORIOL PI-SUNYER
Associate Professor of Anthropology
University of Massachusetts

JOHN WILEY & SONS, INC.
New York · London · Sydney · Toronto

1 2 3 4 5 6 7 8 9 10
Library of Congress Catalog Card Number: 69-16042
Cloth: SBN 471 20210 x Paper: SBN 471 20211 8
Printed in the United States of America

Preface

The changing terminology that we use to describe nonindustrial nations—backward, underdeveloped, and developing—is in itself indicative of changing values and attitudes toward these conditions and levels of economic performance. While it is true that under colonial tutelage there was a concern to bring the blessings of Christianity and commerce to less-favored peoples, this was conceived primarily in terms of slightly improved economic activity, expanded craft production, stabilized food supply, and financial self-sufficiency. Unfortunately, many nations have not attained these modest accomplishments. Whatever could be said of the necessity for achieving these goals as a platform for further change, it is clear that they fall far short of the aspirations and needs of our time. In the first chapter we attempt to chronicle some of the political factors that have transformed the idea of development and generated national consciousness. The primary forces engendering this nationalism have been the two World Wars, the participation in them by colonial soldiers, the subsequent Cold War, foreign aid, and the emergence of a "third world" consciousness.

Nationalism and other facets of political life have provided us with the most dramatic episodes of change in developing countries; nevertheless, meaningful change has been occurring in other areas of life, such as agriculture, urbanization, and some industrialization. Despite these changes it is still questionable whether the social and economic theories of the industrial countries are relevant to an understanding of tribal or peasant communities. In Chapter II we explore that question and then proceed to analyze tribal and peasant life and the cultural factors that at times limit the potential for economic change. Even with the rapid urbanization of recent years, tribesmen and peasants still form the overwhelming majority of the

v

population of developing areas. Consequently, meaningful economic development can only occur if the motives and restraints of these people are fully understood, both by local planners and foreign economic advisers. Therefore, in Chapter IV we investigate the important relationship between peasant villages and national life. Special attention is given here to the study of class, caste, and lineage systems, and their flexibility (or lack of it) in the face of otherwise favorable opportunities for economic change.

The growth of nationalism since World War II and the subsequent achievement of independence by a vast number of nations have not only altered the concept of underdevelopment but have also affected our ideas of what can be done about it. Traditional ideas of the central importance of financial considerations have had to be scrapped or at least drastically modified. Financial aid has proved inadequate to trigger a significant improvement in economic performance. Despite the persistence of take-off theories that focus on the rate of saving, economists have increasingly been examining technological and cultural factors to aid in understanding both the Western economic experience as well as that of the developing areas. Economists and the International Bank now speak of the "absorptive capacity" of an economy. While absorptive capacity does not provide an explanation, it directs us to investigate the level of education and skills, the existing complement of tools, technology, and other facets of the infrastructure, and the cultural forces that would strengthen or retard the introduction of a new technology. In Chapter III we look at the absorptive capacity of the agricultural sector, and in Chapter V we examine the character of urban education, the skills of the labor force, and the problem of unskilled labor, that is, the culture of poverty.

In studying agriculture we study the whole question of the ecology of the transference of crops and agricultural techniques. Crops and techniques are products of a given environment and cultural ecology; to be diffused to other areas, modification must occur so that the innovation will "fit" into the new complex and the cultural restraint will be minimized. With this in mind, we survey traditional agricultural forms, hoe and shifting cultivation, and peasant and other more settled forms of cultivation of food sources—arboreal or aquatic. Then, in terms of these established forms, we look at the potential of modern science and technology to transform them.

In sub-Saharan Africa, urbanization is a relatively new phenomenon, while in Asia and Latin America it is deeply rooted in both indigenous traditional cities and administrative and commercial centers brought about by European contact and control. These centers have been an important source for nationalism and modernization. Since they have been influenced strongly by European established educational institutions and by the transference of attitudes from colonial administrators to the new local elites, we study in Chapter V the evolution of educational institutions in Europe and in the developing areas, and then we evaluate the relevance of this education for the tasks of economic development. Equally important in our study is the learning process that workers have acquired by working with complex machinery and by living in a more technological environment, ranging from simple tools to automobiles and electricity. The formation of worker organizations and class consciousness was an important factor in gaining independence and, while of diminished significance today, can nevertheless be a consequential force in the thrust for modernization. Ranking below the organized worker in the economic and social hierarchy are the unskilled laborers who are often ignored by writers of development texts. Our aim in studying the culture of poverty is to focus on one of the problems of development that is most difficult to solve yet is in most dire need of solution.

In formulating their ideas about development, economists and political leaders of developing areas have placed great emphasis on planning. Unfortunately, as we attempt to show in Chapter VI, planning is often a ritual and symbol (but not the substance) of modernization. Meaningful planning is operational planning; it directs human behavior into certain activities and orients the use of science and technology toward an improvement in economic well-being. Since much of the vital science and technology must be imported, at least initially, we look at the structure and potential of exports, particularly raw commodities, and the current level of indebtedness in order to obtain a clearer conception of the real import potential of current exports. We then study project planning, feasibility studies, and in general the need for coordinated planning both for continued development and for technological leadership to be sustained. In our view, coordinated planning must encompass and reflect an understanding of cultural, political, and technological, as well as economic, factors in order to be effective and not falter as a result of a failure to include exogenous or noneconomic variables. While it is not possible for the student of development to be fully knowledgeable in all the disciplines that would be required for such a breadth of understanding, the development economists should at least have a notion of the forces that will influence planning and the sources of information that would aid in overcoming threatened obstacles. We hope that in some way we have contributed to this objective of an integrated interdisciplinary approach to the enterprise of economic development.

Thomas R. De Gregori
Oriol Pi-Sunyer

Contents

Chapter IV
PEASANT VILLAGE AND NATIONAL CULTURE

Chapter V
URBANIZATION, EDUCATION, AND DEVELOPMENT

Chapter VI
DEVELOPMENT PLANNING

ECONOMIC DEVELOPMENT:
THE CULTURAL CONTEXT

I

The Concept of Underdevelopment

THE ENDING OF COLONIALISM

For some time now, social scientists have recognized that the concept of on-going economic and social change is foreign to most preindustrial societies. We are informed, for instance, that for the most part

These were societies with hereditary hierarchial rule, living under the sway of customs rather than law. Their economies were static and remained at the same level of limited technology and low income from one generation to the next. Even though some ancient societies exhibited high proficiency in certain directions, they should be termed traditional since they were incapable of generating a regular flow of inventions and of moving into a phase of sustained economic growth.[1]

While not all preindustrial societies exhibit the same degree of conservatism, the concept of sustained economic development and accompanying social change is essentially foreign to traditional society. Somewhat less obvious, but equally important, is the fact that the politico-economic concept of an "underdeveloped world," with all that this implies in terms of responsibilities for advanced

[1] Max F. Millikan and Donald L. M. Blackmer, *The Emerging Nations: Their Growth and United States Policy*, Cambridge, Mass., 1961, p. 3.

1

nations, is itself of recent origin. Consequently, we must balance the disinclination of traditional societies to undergo change with the not altogether welcome realization on the part of the developed world that it is expected to underwrite the tasks of transformation.

Of course, men have for many centuries recognized the existence of relative degrees of economic complexity in human societies. Our Victorian forefathers certainly distinguished between "backward" lands and those that were technologically more advanced, while in their day Roman bureaucrats kept careful tally of the industrial and agricultural outputs of the various provinces and had a fair idea of the economic organization of areas beyond the imperial frontiers. The novelty lies not in the condition of underdevelopment—although it should be noted that the term itself implies the absence of something desirable and is of recent coinage—but in the growing recognition that the economic vicissitudes of less favored or less developed areas are matters of concern to a wider audience, not just to the rulers of regions and countries in question.

A number of factors are responsible for this new awareness. Modern technology is steadily eroding the barriers of time and space; and while this does not necessarily make for greater understanding, it does make for propinquity. The problems of the underdeveloped world have called for attention as a consequence of two complementary historical trends: the decline of traditional imperial systems and the polarization of the technologically advanced nations into competing camps.

Some historians trace the origins of imperial decline to the terminal years of the nineteenth century, or at least to the cataclysmic events of the First World War. Certainly, a good case can be argued that the late nineteenth century represents the Indian summer of European power, a time when Europe, and especially Britain, was living on the accumulated credit of past achievements. Correct as this interpretation may be, the realities of power do not always manifest themselves immediately. World War I, destructive and debilitating though it was for European nations, was still a "limited" war, restricted for the most part to Europe and the Near East. The rest of the world remained virtually untouched, and it must have appeared to most observers in 1918 that the formal structure of imperial control had survived unchallenged. True, some territories changed hands, but it was in the main a case of new rulers, not new systems.

Also, the two major powers destined to play critical roles in the years following the Second World War remained pretty much offstage: the Soviet Union, concerned with internal consolidation following a bloody civil war; the United States, limited in her influence by the resurgence of traditional isolationism.

Britain and France, as victor nations, emerged from Versailles with their empires augmented by League of Nations Trust Territories and Mandates in Africa and the Middle East. In the Far East, Japan retained control of Korea and Formosa, brought under her control some former German holdings in the Pacific, and soon made good her claims to Manchuria. The China of the 1920's and 1930's was still very much the China of the Treaty Ports and the Foreign Concessions. In the Western Hemisphere, the hegemony of the United States over the Caribbean republics was perpetuated well into the 1930's.

It would be incorrect to imply that the underdeveloped world, and in particular the dependent territories, failed to be affected by the changes, disturbances, and reorientations experienced by the major powers in the first quarter of this century. But the influences were for the most part indirect, shown more by the uncertainty and questioning of established values by the peoples of Europe and America than by tangible changes in the underdeveloped world.[2] Thus, nationalism in the old imperial holdings was barely beginning to make itself felt. In British India, it took the form of a divided groundswell that could still be controlled through conventional police methods backstopped by no more than thirty British infantry battalions—hardly a major internal security problem. Nationalism was also a nascent force in the Middle East, the Maghreb, and the Phillippines. In Africa south of the Sahara nationalism was little more than the dream of a minuscule number of Western educated Africans. Nationalistic elements were present in Indochina, the Dutch East Indies, and other regions of Southeast Asia, but in the main these were disorganized manifestations still lacking a solid base of popular support.

If the First World War and the interwar years sapped the will and strength of metropolitan powers, the Second World War dealt the mortal blow to empire. In a manner quite unlike the Great War of the previous generation, it was a genuinely global holocaust which not only temporarily shattered continental Europe from the Atlantic

[2] There were, of course, some critical social and political shifts in the underdeveloped world. The 1910 Mexican Revolution and the overthrow of the Manchu dynasty in China one year later were certainly irreversible shifts. It was also in the first quarter of the century that the Indian Congress Party began to move in the direction of independence.

to the Volga, but also ranged far afield to encompass campaigns in Africa, the Pacific, and Asia. A characteristic aspect of the war fought in these extra-European regions was the clear incapacity of the old imperial powers to defend their overseas possessions. In a series of remarkably swift campaigns, the Japanese made themselves masters of vast portions of the Pacific and Southeast Asia; North Africa was for four years the battleground of contending armies; the Levant witnessed the spectacle of British forces—in large part Indian troops —campaigning against French colonial garrisons.

The Japanese assault on European colonies was especially devastating. It demonstrated to the local inhabitants that European arms were by no means invincible, and it also underscored the fact that in the twentieth century industrialization was a prerequisite for national sovereignty and independent action. The fall of France in 1940 and the German occupation of Holland and Belgium left the overseas territories of these nations stripped of homeland support. While the British Isles remained defiant and unconquered, the pressures of war in the West greatly weakened the British presence east of Suez and showed that a Royal Navy heavily committed to an Atlantic battle for survival could no longer defend and protect British possessions in the East.

It is true that American power in the Pacific also suffered grave temporary setbacks, but in this case the political and military repercussions were less severe. Guam, Wake, and the Philippines fell to Japanese forces, but these were outposts and territories peripheral to American war-making capacity. Furthermore, the promise of Philippine independence and its implementation immediately after the war (July 4, 1946) formally withdrew the United States from the ranks of the major colonial powers.

During the war, and in the years following it, the Western allies found themselves increasingly dependent on American economic aid and military support. By 1947 it was evident that in the West the United States was the only great power. Britain found herself no longer capable of carrying the financial burden imposed by support of the anti-Communist government in the Greek civil war, and France was already beginning to lose the first Vietnamese war. It was, in fact, the economic difficulties of her recent allies and the general destruction in continental Europe that necessitated the launching of an American-financed program of recovery, the Marshall Plan (or to give it its full title, the European Recovery Program). While it was not apparent at the time, this scheme was to pave the way for other American postwar aid ventures.

If the military and economic decline of the western European powers made the reconstitution of postwar imperial systems a doubtful project, the acceleration of indigenous nationalism imposed a premium on colonial rebuilding that these powers were either unwilling or unable to meet. Rather precipitously, Britain granted independence to India and Pakistan—the first of over a score of colonies destined to follow the same path. This process of devolution certainly did not go unchallenged. France and the Netherlands initially refused to bend to the winds of change, but eventually nationalistic revolution, coupled with homeland disenchantment over imperial burdens, underscored the inevitability of change.

Another force working in the direction of decolonization was the very values in whose name the war had been fought. While some European politicians might, and did, maintain that declarations such as the Atlantic Charter were to be read as covering only the freedoms of previously sovereign states, it was nevertheless grossly inconsistent to espouse a world order in which self-determination was limited to some nations and some portions of the globe.

Again, the establishment of centers of resistance in overseas territories, such as the Free French enclave in Equatorial Africa and the recruitment of troops from among the indigenous populations, could hardly help but acquaint colonial subjects with the conduct of modern war.[3] Mention might also be made of the postwar French policy of using Algerian, Moroccan, and other colonial troops in Indochina. If Japanese victory in the early 1940's showed that Asians could defeat Europeans, the French collapse at Dienbienphu proved beyond doubt that a colonial people could successfully wage war against an industrial, if albeit demoralized, modern state. This lesson was not lost to repatriated colonial soldiers.

Affecting these trends were the policies and sentiments of the United States. During the war, and in the years following it, American policy with respect to questions of colonialism had not been altogether consistent. In the main, though, independence movements could count on a degree of tacit American support. The United States was instrumental in persuading the Dutch to grant independence to Indonesia and later to cede western New Guinea (West Irian) to that country. On the whole too, American pressures on France acted to facilitate independence for North African territories. It must be remembered that anti colonialism, perhaps especially anti-British-

[3] As a case in point, Ferhat Abbas, Mohammed Ben Bella, and Belkacem Krim, key leaders of the Algerian revolution, all had seen service in the French army.

colonialism, enjoyed a broad appeal in the America of the 1930's and the 1940's and that to a considerable degree popular opinion was reflected in official action. It is perhaps especially germane today to remember that President Franklin D. Roosevelt's profound distaste for the French in Indochina left the colony open to Japanese invasion and later doomed Free French efforts to launch an anti-Japanese resistance movement. The President's antipathy, in fact, encompassed virtually all imperial powers, an attitude that is evident in the evaluation of the causes of the war in the Pacific which he offered to his son Elliott in 1942: "Don't think for a moment . . . that Americans would be dying tonight, if it had not been for the short-sighted greed of the French, the British and the Dutch."[4]

Given the general economic frailty of the Western European allies, and the longing for peace following half a decade of war on the part of the inhabitants of these countries, major colonial wars without strong American support were in the long run bound to fail. The United States, though, ended the war with its own share of colonial and neocolonial problems. These burdens were substantially lightened with the granting of independence to the Philippines and the passage of a new constitution for Puerto Rico defining its relationship to the Federal Government as that of an Associated State ("Commonwealth" in the favored English rendition). Nevertheless, the onus of colonialism was not so easily lifted. Latin Americans in particular are well aware of the fact that throughout this century the United States has exercised what can only be termed a protectorate over Latin America. The American exercise of power, evident in military intervention and occupation (Nicaragua, Mexico, Haiti, Santo Domingo), the acquisition of military bases (Cuba, Panama), and various instances of fiscal control and customs receiverships were predicated on the Monroe Doctrine and the Roosevelt (Theodore) corollary to it that the "Monroe Doctrine may force the United States . . . . to the exercise of an international police power." These rights of intervention and interposition, being strictly unilateral, have never commended themselves to the peoples of Latin America or to their governments.

It is certainly correct to note that by 1939 American quasi-suzerainty in Latin America had passed its crest and that American foreign policy in the area increasingly relied on persuasion rather than force. Nevertheless, postwar events have not always been calculated to add lustre to the American image. The Bay of Pigs fiasco and the Marine landings in the Dominican Republic raised afresh well

[4] Elliott Roosevelt, *As He Saw It*, New York, 1945, p. 115.

developed Latin American fears of unilateral American action. In the latter event, the United States acted first and only later tried to elicit the support of the Organization of American States. The Panama Canal question continues to vex American-Panamanian relations, and only a few years ago (1964) Panama threatened to bring the issue to the United Nations if certain basic Panamanian demands on the status of the canal and sovereignty over the Zone were not successfully negotiated. As this is written, diplomacy is still at work, but no mutually acceptable solution has yet been reached.

American anticolonialism—certainly a genuine element in the political makeup of the nation—must therefore be balanced against a history of colonial involvement and hemispheric intervention. Consequently, it is understandable that the intentions of the United States do not always go unquestioned. The issue of colonialism is complicated by the fact that in the modern world colonialism is often taken to encompass areas of activity and forms of influence substantially broader in scope than territorial aggrandisement. Economic preponderance has the potential of being used as a more or less covert instrument of policy. Thus, within the hemisphere, the United States is so strong, economically so dominant, that at times it has been viewed by neighboring nations—Canada as well as Latin America—as posing a threat to independent national action.

But beyond fears of economic domination there lie anxieties concerning cultural domination. This is the theme of one of President Sukarno's exhortations to the young.

And you, young men and young women, you who are certainly against economic imperialism and oppose economic imperialism, you who oppose political imperialism—why is it that amongst you many do not oppose cultural imperialism? Why is that amongst you many still like to indulge in rock'n roll, to "dance" à la cha-cha-cha, to make crazy mixed up noises called music, and more of the same?

Why is it that amongst you many like to read foreign writings which are clearly cultural imperialism? The Government will protect our national culture, but you, young men and young women, you must also join actively in opposing cultural imperialism, and in protecting and developing our National culture![5]

Strange this fear of imperialism compounded of Coca-Cola, miniskirts, and the latest records of the hit parade; much harder for us to understand than fears of political domination and of overriding

[5] President Sukarno, *Towards Freedom and the Dignity of Man*, Djakarta, 1961, p. 65.

economic influence. Nevertheless, reactions of this type have manifested themselves not only in Sukarno's Indonesia—where as the result of bloody revolt and bloodier counter-coup the target is now Chinese culture and the overseas Chinese minority—but in such desperate regimes as Diem's Vietnam, Mao's China, the Cuba of Fidel Castro, and the current Greek military government. There is a strand of unity that links all these manifestations, although to what degree they reflect popular feeling as distinct from official antipathy is hard to ascertain. Again, the thread appears to be primarily nationalism. True, not all developing countries equally share nightmares of foreign domination, of external cultural intrusion and the displacement of national culture, but the theme is common enough to warrant consideration

✓ Perhaps all nationalism, old and new, is in part founded on the sometimes uncritical rejection of the foreign. During the romantic period in Europe, nationalists stressed the virtues of the native tongue, the desirability of giving new lease to native values and native culture. The intense emotional symbolism of language is illustrated in the actions and behavior of Magyar nobles sitting in the newly-constituted Hungarian parliament. Lacking fluency in Hungarian—for by the early nineteenth century Hungarian had been reduced to the speech of the peasantry—and unwilling to discourse in German, these gentlemen were forced to conduct their business in Latin. Today, we find reflections of this attitude in the resistance that Hindi is meeting in southern India. Parliamentarians from the south much prefer to use English, which, if nothing else, is a commentary on the passing of the British Raj.

But historical analogy only carries us so far. Many underdeveloped countries, especially those of Asia and Africa, have only recently achieved political independence. For a period prior to independence, Western culture, in the broadest sense, was viewed with favor by the rising colonial elites as a potential avenue to modernization. By and large, these men consciously modeled themselves on the Europeans with whom they came into contact, a transformation which, initially at least, found support among colonial administrators. This shift—this "Westernization," as it was sometimes called—was much more than the copying of external patterns. It included changes in values and attitudes and an acceptance of Western social and political ideals. But these ideals, colonials soon realized, were not to find expression in their territories. Native education had its place in the colonial scheme of things, so long as it made available a corps of trained subordinates to man the civil service, the

schools, the commercial establishments, and the various other structures of colonial society. Education, though, entailed much more
than the learning of skills. It involved the exposure of subject peoples
to the great egalitarian traditions of Europe and their contemporary
political manifestations. Some colonial powers, Belgium is a good
example, attempted to reduce the incompatibility inherent in the
combination of European education and colonial status. The Belgian
formula rested on an artificial ceiling on native education: the Congo
had, comparatively, fine primary schools, virtually no secondary
schools, and certainly no university facilities. Neither France nor
Britain opted for such a solution, a solution that later events proved
was illusionary. Britain hoped that its native elites would emulate
the forms of its own apolitical civil service, while France aimed at a
piecemeal incorporation of "evolved" colonials into the mainstream
of French intellectual life. In both cases, some success is attributable
to these policies. In India especially, the British were able to establish
competent and professional organs of administration, a civil service,
a judiciary, and a police and military establishment, all essentially
removed from political influences. The French doctrine of assimilation offered the privileges of French culture, and even participation
in French political life, to a select few from the colonies.

The ultimate failure of these experiments rested in part on the
relatively few positions of trust and influence that the colonial
systems made available to local talent, but mostly on the failure of
metropolitan governments to meet the political expectations of dependent peoples. In the colonial situation the citizen enjoyed few
if any political rights. Administration might be more or less good—
in some cases certainly superior to that of contemporary successor
states—but political participation at a level above local bodies
(regional, municipal, etc.) was virtually nonexistent. Apparently it
was fine for Frenchmen to espouse the teachings of Thomas Paine,
but the human rights gained by the French Revolution were not
generally to be read as applying to overseas territories; an Englishman
might well boast of traditional English freedoms enshrined in Magna
Carta, Petition of Rights, and Reform Laws, but again these doctrines
were not for the most part applicable to subjects outside the British
Isles—excepting, of course, the fortunate few in the white Commonwealth.

It is hardly surprising, therefore, that the hopes and expectations
of an emerging educated class were destined to turn into frustration
and rejection. Colonial governments did make concessions—Indian
provinces were granted internal autonomy in 1937; as early as 1848

France granted full rights of citizenship to the inhabitants of the four communes of Senegal—but generally such concessions were too little, too late, and more the products of necessity than of a disinterested concern for the welfare of colonial peoples.

The disenchantment of native intellectuals produced reactions on the part of those responsible for colonial administration, which virtually guaranteed a further deterioration in the relationships between rulers and the emerging elites. Pressure from educated and vocal minorities simply reinforced the bias of the colonial power structure to deal with and rely upon traditional indigenous structures and hierarchies. Initially, there may have been no alternative other than the utilization of traditional systems, but this necessity was soon transformed into a virtue. Also, it is probably fair to say that most colonial officials felt more at home in the company of village councils, tribal elders, and native princes than in that of Western-educated Asians and Africans.

Indirect rule, as the system of control through traditional authorities was termed, offered few opportunities for the secondary school and university graduate. It is almost as though through education these men had worked themselves out of a meaningful role in the affairs of their own society. In short, effort and sacrifice closed the doors of traditional society without opening alternative avenues. What posts were available to the educated man in the colonial situation demanded something approaching an absolute commitment to the values, attitudes, and general style of life of the governing group. No such demand was required of those positioned in traditional society. Furthermore, as many were to learn by bitter experience, assimilation or integration must necessarily be a two-way street; regardless of formal credentials—the university degree, the civil service posting, the military commission—Europeans were seldom prone to grant social or intellectual equality to colonial subjects. Among many other failings and shortcomings, it may be remarked that in this century (it is too much to expect it of the last) European powers missed the opportunity to nurture in their possessions the spirit of a loyal opposition which in due course might have taken on the responsibilities of sovereign government. To the degree that efforts were made in this direction, such as in British India, the transference of power was facilitated and relatively stable administrations emerged with independence. But the agonies of postcolonial experience prove how little headway was made in most colonial territories.

Naturally, this failure on the part of colonial rulers to recognize that men, disenchanted with a system of life and government, will strive for an alternative, simply added thrust to movements of national independence. While the details vary, nationalistic manifestations were characterized by features reflecting the colonial experience. Thus, unlike nationalism in nineteenth-century Europe, it is seldom that one encounters conscious attempts to build on old traditions. European intellectuals looked for the mainsprings of a national identity in peasant and folk societies, the sectors of the population that had most successfully resisted the encroachment of foreign ways. There is, of course, some use made of traditional symbolic forms by the governing elites of emerging countries. Jomo Kenyatta, a man very much the product of the London School of Economics, is not to be seen without his fly whisk, a badge of chieftainship in East Africa; members of the Congress Party in India still dress in homespun cotton, indicative of a link with the peasantry. But the emphasis is more on modernization than on the remembrance of things past. In fact, it is no exaggeration that the newly independent countries have witnessed a greater erosion of traditional authority in the past fifteen years than in the preceeding century. One might say that a double rejection is involved: colonialism in all its facets, and the traditional structures which, it is felt, proved themselves all too ready to cooperate in schemes of colonial domination.

The evolution of national identity in former dependent territories can be traced in the nomenclature of political and social associations. Initially—in the decade of the thirties for the most part—such associations as existed tended to be either tribal in nature or limited to specific individuals with limited interests or special credentials: literary clubs, associations of graduates, and so forth. In many cases, associations of this type eventually formed themselves into loose groupings of a more universal nature. The terms that these bodies used to describe themselves—"Convention," "Congress," "*Ressemblement*," "Council," and the like—indicate that the organizations aimed to express something approaching national consensus. At this level, concern was mainly with internal questions, including matters of franchise and representation, but not necessarily autonomy and independence. In the years preceeding independence, the wartime years and the postwar era, the goals of political associations become increasingly those of independence. In some instances, association labels remain unchanged, but increasingly the term "party" comes into vogue, at times in tandem with older terms such as in the case of the Gold Coast (Ghana) Convention People's Party. Paralleling these developments was a tendency for colonial organizations such as trade unions and political parties to sever their ties with metropolitan bodies.

These shifts were a necessary prelude to independence. Internally, they provided organizational experience for the nationalist leadership. The broadening of the base of participation to include as much as possible of the educated, organized, and modern-oriented sectors of the population gave weight to the claim that the organizations in question represented the nation in being, and not simply a small group of malcontents without following.

THE COLD WAR AND THE THIRD WORLD

If nationalism and imperial decline constitute one strand of the postwar situation, the confrontation—ranging from hot "cold war" to competitive coexistence—between communist nations and the bulk of the developed countries of the West represents an equally important reference point. It is not that poverty, underdevelopment, and nationalism are in any way products of ideological conflict, but rather that this conflict imposes itself on the foreign policies of both developed and underdeveloped countries.

In the contemporary jargon it is common to speak of a "third" world. Depending on the speaker and the circumstances, the term can either signify essentially nonaligned (what in an earlier generation would have been called "neutral") nations, or nations that have yet to join the ranks of the technologically developed. In many instances, although by no means all, there occurs a coincidence of meaning: underdeveloped countries, especially those that have achieved independence in the course of the last two decades, have tended to remain outside the political orbits of the two major world powers, the United States and Russia, and their respective blocs and allies.

There are some very pragmatic reasons for this stance. Most third world leaders believe that the avoidance of a major clash between East and West is the *minimal* precondition for their economic and technological advancement; war and preparations for war cannot but cut deeply into funds which might otherwise be available for overseas development. Also—as was shown during the Second World War—

policies of nonalignment are hard to maintain during a global conflict; the pressures to take sides or bear the consequences are simply too strong. The countries of the developing world have no wish to be forced into the dilemma of a choice, a choice which, once made, automatically reduces their influence, an influence that is much less based on economic or military power than on the fact that the underdeveloped world speaks for a large segment of humanity. As Jawaharlal Nehru said shortly before his death:

Our capacity is limited, but we have a certain capacity, a certain strength, call it what you like, moral strength, or other strength. Let us use it properly, rightly, without force but with courtesy and with a friendly approach so that we may influence those who have the power of war and peace in their hands. . . .[6]

Not all third world countries are unaligned, nor are all unaligned countries economically underdeveloped. Some technologically advanced nations, either in keeping with traditional policies or as a consequence of postwar settlements, have followed a course of neutrality. Sweden and Switzerland have made neutrality the touchstone of their foreign policy in every world and European conflict since Napoleonic times, while the nonaligned policies of Finland and Austria are linked to specific clauses in post-World War II peace treaties. It should also be noted that the reduction of tensions along what was once referred to as the "iron curtain" has permitted experiments in foreign policy mobility by countries on both sides of the ideological divide.

Conversely, quite a number of underdeveloped countries have cut the sails of their neutrality to ride the political storms of the cold war. Nevertheless, to the degree that there is an element of general policy or, more accurately, a policy ideal, in the third world it is in the direction of nonalignment. Such policies appear to have a better chance of survival in regions peripheral to major power confrontations, newly independent Africa being perhaps the best contemporary example.

The pressures along the Southeast Asian periphery have, on the other hand, made the implementation of truly independent policies extremely difficult. This is true not only for the Indochinese cockpit (where nevertheless the goal of an independent foreign policy finds favor in the official communiques of the governments of North and South Vietnam, as well as those of Cambodia and Laos), but for

[6] *The Conference of Heads of State or Government of Nonaligned Countries*, Belgrade, 1961, p. 117.

adjacent lands as well. Thus India, while strongly protesting the virtues of nonalignment, has been forced to call for help in the face of military pressures from its former Bandung partner across the Himalayas. Pakistan has also adjusted her policies, but as might be expected, given mutual antagonisms with India, in an entirely different direction. Of all the southern Asian countries, only Burma has consistently been willing to pay the price of absolute nonalignment, but whatever the political profits may turn out to be, the retardation of economic growth through lack of sustained cooperation with technologically advanced nations is at least partially a consequence of this policy.

FOREIGN AID AND DEVELOPMENT: THE BURMESE CASE

Burma, in fact, is an excellent case study of the economic and political problems faced by underdeveloped countries in the context of the sometimes direct, more often indirect, struggle between the power blocs. It is not so much that the Burmese solution of what adds up to almost total disengagement is typical of the options followed by most developing countries—the Burmese fear of involvement is in fact extreme—but rather that the Burmese have reacted so strongly to dangers generally recognized throughout the third world.

Burma, as was the case with many countries in the region, came out of the war with a shattered economy. According to an economist involved in postwar American aid programs, the war "destroyed a larger share of the nation's physical wealth than was destroyed in any other country of the world except perhaps Greece."[7] The task of reconstruction would require long-term financial assistance and massive technical aid, help which only the technologically advanced nations, in particular the United States, were in a position to provide. Aid programs, though, were developing in the context of the sharpening cold war situation (the period of the Berlin air lift and Korea, the Greek civil war and pressures on Turkey and Iran) and also coincided with a spate of internal revolts and dislocations within Burma itself. Understandably, the Burmese were sensitive, perhaps over-sensitive, to ideological implications entailed in aid programs.

[7] Everett E. Hagen, *The Economic Development of Burma*, Washington, D.C., 1956, p. 31.

The history of foreign aid operations in Burma is too complex to examine in detail, but a few events and situations will serve to sketch the mood of the times. When, early in 1952, the Economic Development Administration was renamed the Mutual Security Agency, the Burmese press, shortly followed by the Burmese government, concluded that the acceptance of American aid would jeopardize Burmese freedom of action in the formulation of foreign policy. In this instance, American flexibility and goodwill, evident in the readiness to change the name of the local agency of MSA to the purely descriptive "Technical and Economic Aid," allowed the rapid resumption of aid measures.

Nevertheless, a year later relations between the two countries became so strained that Burma decided to terminate American programs. The incident that triggered this decision was one that touched both on the cold war and on internal conditions in Burma. Ever since independence, the Burmese government had experienced great difficulty in controlling those parts of Highland Burma inhabited by ethnic minorities with their own regional and nationalistic aspirations. To complicate matters, units of the defeated Chinese Nationalist Army had moved into these unsettled areas following the defeat of the Kuomintang regime. These troops, the Burmese claimed, were receiving aid from Taiwan, and more significantly, from bases established by American intelligence in Thailand. After bringing the issue before the United Nations, Burma declared that she could no longer accept aid from a country that was abetting the operation of forces fighting the Burmease army. For three years virtually all American aid to Burma was suspended.[8]

To meet her foreign aid requirements Burma turned to the Soviet bloc, a move made all the more necessary by a drastic decline in the world price of rice, the country's main source of foreign earnings. Various barter arrangements were entered into, but these plans also did not entirely function to the satisfaction of Burmese authorities. In part, it was felt that the quality, cost, and suitability of materials were not up to standard; also, from 1957 onward the price of rice on the world market rose and consequently barter arrangements based on rice were less advantageous.[8]

Eventually American aid was resumed and this, together with aid from the Soviet nations, the Commonwealth, United Nations agencies, and a number of smaller donors, had a valuable—if limited —effect on the Burmese economy.

Strict adherence to nonalignment has remained a constant in

[8] Louis Walinsky, *Economic Development in Burma, 1951–1960*, New York, 1962, pp. 201, 209–210.

Burmese foreign policy through changes in government and periodic shifts from parliamentary to military rule. This policy has allowed Burma to accept aid from all donors without compromise; it has not assured good planning or a brilliant record of economic development. The Burmese government's extreme sensitivity to putative external pressures has led to many programs being abandoned in midstream while others can be more fairly termed a series of unrelated gifts rather than planned courses of development. This fear of involvement, laced with a more than common degree of nationalistic touchiness, has also acted to downgrade technical advice in favor of "hard" aid—the tangibles of buildings, plants, machinery, and communications equipment. Planning, though, requires the type of skilled personnel that is especially rare in the underdeveloped lands. In this context, one may note that the University of Rangoon, the only one in the country, had by 1938–1939 a student body of about 3000, few of them enrolled in the fields of technology, economics, and related areas. In short, an extremely shallow pool of talent from which to recruit all the personnel needed for a program of national development. Inevitably, many false starts were made, and much aid was wasted.

FOREIGN AID: THE ATTITUDES OF THE U.S. AND U.S.S.R.

The Burmese case, while certainly extreme in some respects, is offered as an illustration of just how complex an issue is the transference of aid. In part the lesson is that with the exception of some small donors and international agencies (and then maybe not always) aid entails a tripartite relationship: the formal negotiation and implementation of aid between the donor and the recipient nation, and in the background, the influence of the "other side." Thus, while foreign aid may superficially take on the attributes of a bilateral agreement, the attitudes and motivations of the contracting parties tend to be influenced by the action of forces outside the conference room.

It is a valid objection that aid applied as an instrument of the cold war, a weapon in an ideological struggle, perverts what should in fact be an act of disinterested humanitarianism. Some have professed that the developed countries "owe" the underdeveloped ones the means to achieve industrialization and economic growth, since, after all, it was the developed lands that in the past forcibly penetrated simple and traditional societies and instilled in them—or at least some sectors of them—the appetites for change and progress.

Arguments of this type are especially prevalent among intellectuals and governing entities in the underdeveloped world. Originally, as John S. Bandeau, former United States ambassador to the United Arab Republic, points out, the demand was for political freedom. But now:

there is a new right, the right to technical development and to the assistance necessary for it. No longer are medicine, science, industrial skill, and economic development to be view (sic) as *ex gratia* gifts of the wealthier and more advanced Western World. They are rather an obligation, owed by the world community to the emerging people.[9]

Psychologically this attitude, this belief, is understandable, and morally it has more than an element of credit. Payment, it is felt, should be made for past indignities and exploitations, for colonial control and political domination. There is also the recognition that in today's world true nationhood is incompatible with economic backwardness. More than this, though, gifts place an onerous burden on the recipient; explicitly or otherwise, they entail reciprocity, if only the reciprocity of being beholden to much stronger and richer nations. For the emerging countries, self-consciously nationalistic, defensive with respect to newly minted and often imperfect governmental and administrative structures, the price is a stiff one to pay. How much more satisfying it is to categorize aid as an obligation due rather than a gratuitous favor.

It is not unusual for governments in the developed world to invoke an element of duty as a contributory factor in foreign assistance programs. In his inaugural address, the late President John F. Kennedy said:

To those peoples in the huts and villages of half the globe struggling to break the bonds of mass misery, we pledge our best efforts to help them help themselves for whatever period is required—not because the Communists may be doing it, not because we seek their votes, but because it is right. If a free society cannot help the many who are poor, it cannot save the few who are rich.

These are very stirring words, but on the whole there has been strong resistance, especially by the legislative branch of the United States government, to aid as a moral obligation or to open-ended commit-

[9] John S. Bandeau, "Development and Diplomacy in the Middle East," *Bulletin of the Atomic Scientists*, Vol. XXII, No. 5, May 1966, p. 6.

ments ("for whatever period is required"). In 1954 the report of the Commission on Foreign Economic Policy (the Randall Report) categorically expressed the opinion that "underdeveloped areas are claiming the right to economic aid from the United States. . . . We recognize no such right." There is little reason to doubt that this continues to be the overwhelming temper of Congress. Some of the commentary from the Soviet Union has much the same ring, which is not so surprising, since both countries carry heavy defense expenditures and must move toward meeting growing domestic social demands. Thus, a few years ago Nikolai Federenko, head of the permanent mission of the U.S.S.R. to the United Nations, indicated that while the Soviet Union was willing to extend economic aid to developing countries (the specific reference is to Africa, but the sentiments surely apply to other areas),

This problem is not of our doing, the moral and material responsibility is not ours, either before the African peoples or before history.[10]

In a later section of the speech, Federenko blames economic backwardness on colonialism and neocolonialism and asserts that the responsibility for change falls squarely on the shoulders of the West. Aid from the Soviet camp is a gesture of friendship, not a response to obligations incurred by past actions. The underdeveloped countries, which for the most part are impressed by relative levels of development rather than by the political and ideological distinctions that set apart two portions of the developed world, are unlikely to draw much satisfaction, or much hope, from such arguments

Nations and governments being what they are, it is probably wishful thinking to expect the major impetus behind great foreign aid expenditures to reside in other than self-interest, enlightened, perhaps, but still self-interest. This is not to deny that secondary considerations play a part in the relationships between advanced nations and developing ones. Traditional friendships and cultural affinities can add substantial weight to the primary motivation. In this category would fall British and Commonwealth efforts implemented within the framework of the Colombo Plan and similar schemes, French aid to its former dependencies in Africa, and some United States aid ventures in Latin America. Even in these cases, though, it is worth bearing in mind that aid tends to gravitate to areas in which the

[10] Nikolai Federenko, "The Soviet Union and African Countries," *The Annals of the American Academy of Political and Social Science,* Vol. 254, July 1964, p. 5.

developed countries already have strong political, military, or economic interests.

The claim that aid and the national interests of the donor tend to be closely related can be documented without much trouble. Currently, some 80 percent of United States economic assistance is being expended among the nations of the South and Southeast Asian rim—the same region in which the cold war has shown an increasing propensity to evolve into an outright shooting war. Soviet bloc aid, for its part, has generally tended to manifest itself at such times and locations as appear to offer opportunities for propaganda or more immediate politico-military gains. Cases in point are the Middle East and Indonesia.

There is also a tendency to present aid as part of a package together with military and ideological components. The linkage of military aid and economic assistance no doubt causes some discomfort in the underdeveloped world. A case can be argued, though, that as far as American assistance is concerned, separation of the two would result in lower levels of expenditure for development programs. In 1965 the Chairman of the Committee on Foreign Affairs of the House of Representatives stated:

I feel very strongly the economic program would suffer terrific cuts in the House if military assistance was not tied to it. The military assistance is popular in the House. There are few cuts in it. . . . Many members of the committee who have been around a long time realize that if the separation of the program occurs the economic part is going to suffer. . . . As long as we have military assistance, we should wrap it in the AID package. It has a strong influence in helping put the program through the House.[11]

There is also considerable pressure in Congress to utilize foreign aid as a foreign policy tool in support of American private investment in underdeveloped areas. Foreign assistance is, of course, transacted on a government-to-government basis. Most businessmen recognize the importance of economic development and planning in that it creates an infrastructure within which their enterprises can more effectively operate. In the event of nationalization or expropriation without prompt and adequate compensation, the Hickenlooper Amendment of the Foreign Assistance Act of 1962 provides for the severance within six months of United States foreign as-

[11] Representative Thomas E. Morgan, *Hearings Before the Committee on Foreign Affairs House of Representatives, Eighty-Ninth Congress, Foreign Assistance Act of 1965*, Part VII, U.S. Government Printing Office, Washington, D.C., 1965.

sistance.[12] The whole question of expropriation and nationalization is left somewhat vague in international law. The General Assembly's Declaration on Permanent Sovereignty over National Resources recognizes the sovereign power of governments to control their national economic patrimony, but at the same time calls on nations carrying out an act of nationalization to pay appropriate compensation in accordance with the rules in force in the state taking such measures and in accordance with international law. Clearly, there is room for differences in interpretation.

Soviet aid is also not without its military and ideological strings. In this instance the legislative arrangements need not concern us as it is simply a case of executive decisions obtaining quasi-representative approval. One observes the same linkage of military and economic programs, not perhaps as part of a formal package, but nevertheless in tandem. Ideological overtones are not absent, for there are implicit, and at times explicit, promotions of specific economic solutions, solutions on the Soviet model.

CONCLUSION: CURRENT COLD WAR CONDITIONS

Although ideological and economic confrontation is still very much with us, the resurgence of European nationalism and the economic reconstruction of both East and West have substantially eroded the influence of the two super powers. At the same time, and to some degree as a reflection of these changes, the United States and Russia have made definite efforts in the direction of a *modus vivendi*. This *détente* is something of a surprising phenomenon when we consider that major military operations in Vietnam engage the efforts of 525,000 American troops and that a Russian ally, North Vietnam, is under constant bombardment. It is almost as if the two great powers had evolved a body of rules of international behavior stipulating areas of conflict while permitting the lowering of tension in other spheres.

The pattern emerging is still far from clear, but some broad

[12] Marvin D. Bernstein, " 'We have a sovereign right to protect our investors abroad': A Case and a Commentary," *Foreign Investment in Latin America, Cases and Attitudes*, Marvin D. Bernstein, ed., New York, 1966, pp. 186–211.

trends are identifiable. Obviously, and to the degree that such matters fall within the category of coexistence, the underdeveloped countries can be more flexible in their relationships with both East and West. Increasingly, the acceptance of aid from either camp can be accomplished without the appearance or necessity of ideological commitment: Egypt can openly take Yugoslavia as a model without arousing too much consternation in the West and, similarly, a number of African countries have maintained close cultural, economic, political, and even military ties to France and retained a high degree of freedom of action in their associations with other countries.

At the same time the general decrease in tension between the Soviet Union and the United States has permitted an element of tacit cooperation by the countries on questions affecting the underdeveloped world. In the political sphere, parallel action during the recent India-Pakistan border conflict was certainly instrumental in terminating the fighting. Currently, both countries are engaged in grain shipments to India and other forms of technical assistance. Potentially, cooperative aid ventures could prove to be a major force for development. Conversely, some of the advantages that underdeveloped countries have gleaned from East-West frictions may cease to be operative. The alignment on many important international economic issues is being increasingly structured less on the basis of ideology and more on the basis of industrial versus underdeveloped countries. For instance, the 1964 United Nations Conference on Trade and Development and more recent attempts at commodity agreements have indicated that neither the Soviet Union nor the United States is willing to champion the cause of underdeveloped areas when this would prove adverse to their own national economic interests. There is more than a suspicion that developed lands are looking with increasing disfavor on the steady and, to them, the unremitting demands of the underdeveloped world. Certainly, a new toughness in Congress points in this direction.[13]

China's foreign policy has in the meantime become geared to a world view that does not discriminate in essentials between the Soviet Union and the United States. Her attempts to capitalize on the cleavage between the rich and the poor nations, as well as on the presumed Soviet abandonment of revolutionary ideas, have brought her into sharp conflict with her erstwhile allies. To date, Chinese influence has been pretty well contained. She finds herself without allies

---

[13] In 1966, the Administration requested a $3.39 billion aid budget, which was cut back by Congress to $2.94 billion, the lowest appropriation in almost ten years.

in Eastern Europe (the fossilized Stalinist state of Albania excepted); her influence throughout Southeast Asia has declined in the last decade; her presence in Africa is now minimal. Overall, her bid for solidarity with the underdeveloped countries on the basis of past shared humiliations and present poverty has proved far from successful, and it may be expected that without a modern industrial base political leadership will continue to elude her. This is not to deny that China since 1949 has experienced notable successes in economic development, but these must be balanced by equally notable failures and a tendency to aspire to a role not matched by her resources.

BIBLIOGRAPHY*

* This bibliography and the bibliographies at the end of the other chapters are additions to the material cited in the footnotes and constitute readings that we recommend to the student for further study and clarification of the major points presented.

Adams, Richard, et al., *Social Change in Latin America Today: Its Implication for United States Policy*, New York, 1960.

Apter, David E., *Ghana in Transition*, New York, 1963.

Coleman, James S., *Nigeria: Background to Nationalism*, Berkeley and Los Angeles, 1960.

Dean, Vera Michels, *The Nature of the Non-Western World*, New York, 1957.

Diamond, Stanley and Fred G. Burke (eds.), *The Transformation of East Africa: Essays in Political Anthropology*, New York, 1967.

Hatch, John, *A History of Postwar Africa*, New York, 1965.

Hunter, Guy, *The New Societies of Tropical Africa*, London, 1962.

Kilson, Martin, *Political Change in a West African State*, Cambridge, Mass., 1966.

Myrdal, Jan, *Report from a Chinese Village*, New York, 1966.

Penguin African Library—over twenty volumes already published in this series. Most are on current political topics in Africa and are of consistent high quality and reasonable price.

Piel, Gerard, *Science in the Cause of Man*, New York, 1962.

Veliz, Claudio (ed.), *Obstacles to Change in Latin America*, London, 1965.

Wallerstein, Immanuel, *Africa: The Politics of Independence*, New York, 1961.

II

Culture and Economic Change

The relevance of traditional economic theory and the problem of modernization

Economic change can be viewed as a particular facet of a larger cultural transformation. Economies do not change in isolation from other patterned activities characteristic of a particular people, and in the majority of cases significant shifts in other areas of belief, behavior, or social organization will find a reflection in changed economic patterns. For analytical purposes it is valid to focus on that range of activities, organizational forms, and supporting values that we subsume under the rubric of "economics"; it must be kept in mind, however, that economic and technological behavior is fully understandable only in terms of the total social and cultural context.

Societies undergoing transformation must necessarily adjust to new demands and new conditions. Such an adjustment, though, will always be a partial, and not a total, rejection of the past. In culture change, adjustment and reinterpretation are often more important than outright substitution. At the same time, when transformation is radical in nature—as would generally be the case in steps designed to modernize transactional relationships—some cultural features that are clearly incompatible with new demands will have to be jettisoned altogether. What can remain, perhaps in a somewhat altered form, and what must be discarded depends on both the type of change involved and the flexibility of the cultural forms themselves.

The flexibility of what may initially appear to be features contrary to economic development and modernization is illustrated in the case of Japan. Some one hundred years ago certain characteristics of traditional Japanese society were retooled to provide the foundations of modern industrial organization. In essence, what occured is that that samurai code of Bushido, with its strong emphasis on loyalty, obligation, responsibility, and frugality, was spread through other sectors of the population and took on the characteristic of a national political and social ethic. According to Robert N. Bellah:

Though many features of this penetration had economically irrational results, especially when the political motives were purely in the direction of maintaining the *status quo* and keeping a rigid system of social control in effect, to the extent that the result was the encouragement of production, the encouragement of economy, and the development of a dynamic concept of calling, this penetration must be seen as having a strong favorable effect on economic rationalization.[1]

In the balance, a complex of feudal values proved favorable to the rise of industrial society, a consummation which Bellah is right in pointing out "is not what one would necessarily have expected if one extrapolated only from the European material."[2]

Much, of course, has changed in Japan over the past century. Nevertheless, the organization of Japanese industrial society is still substantially different from the norms current in the West. The degree of loyalty to and identification with the firm which is typical of the Japanese employee far surpasses that of his European and American contemporaries. The reciprocal aspects of this pattern assure both worker and executive an element of security which again is in contrast to Western patterns. Jobs are generally total, life-time involvements and are backed by extensive welfare benefits far in excess of those commonly provided by Western enterprises. The system may at times lack flexibility and place too high an emphasis on such factors as seniority, but on the whole it has not undermined Japan's strong competitive position in the world market. Finally, one might note that the Japanese concern for the individual and his welfare—the sense of duty necessarily involves reciprocity—does much to mitigate the anomic and impersonal biases of large-scale organizations.[3]

[1] Robert N. Bellah, *Takaugawa Religion, The Values of Pre-Industrial Japan*, Glencoe, Ill., 1957, pp. 116–117.

[2] *Ibid.*, p. 192.

[3] For further information on Japanese industrialization, see James C. Abegglen, *The Japanese Factory*, Glencoe, Ill., 1958; Douglass G. Haring, "Japanese National Character: Cultural Anthropology, Psychoanalysis and

Certainly, the standards of one culture do not constitute a valid measure or guide for the detailed structural changes that another culture must undergo. Today this is amply illustrated in the field of political organization: emerging nations have in the course of the past twenty years shown a propensity to discard political forms of Western origin. The same must to some degree prove true for economic systems. This is not to deny that the developed world can offer guide lines and expertise, but the economist's models tend to be derived from as restricted a range of experience as are those of the Western politician. This does not mean that the theories of a discipline—economics in this case—are of necessity inapplicable outside the context of their origin. It merely means that social theories have to be modified to fit the conditions under examination. Frequently, if an effort is made to take into account the changed frame of reference, it is possible to separate what is relevant from what is not in terms of problems and conditions peculiar to developing areas. Furthermore—and this is a matter of no little importance—the testing of theories in a new environment may yield information indicative of shortcomings in the theories, even in their original context. It is the rigidity of traditional economics—the propensity to cram evidence into an ethnocentric conceptual mold—that has led Polanyi, Arensberg, and Pearson to caution that "unless we keep to times and regions where price-making markets are extant, economics cannot supply orientation of any value."[4]

The whole question of the applicability of traditional economic concepts to the analysis of non-Western, nonindustrial, peasant, and primitive societies is an issue that has sharply divided the anthropological profession and has led to substantial reappraisal and reexamination on the part of economists. Men of the stature of Raymond Firth and Melville J. Herskovits have insisted on the universality of economic theory; conversely, George Dalton, Marshall D. Sahlins, and others are equally insistent on the need for different tools, and different concepts, better suited to the examination of traditional, primitive, and peasant economic systems.[5]

History," in Haring (ed.), *Personal Character and Cultural Milieu, A Collection of Readings,* New York, 1949; John W. Bennett and I. Ishino, *Paternalism in the Japanese Economy,* Minneapolis, 1963; Ezra F. Vogel, *Japan's New Middle Class,* Berkeley and Los Angeles, 1963.

[4] Karl Polanyi, Conrad M. Arensberg, and Henry W. Pearson, *Trade and Market in the Early Empires,* New York, 1965, p. 241.

[5] The literature on the question is extensive. For a start, the reader may consult: Melville J. Herskovits, *Economic Anthropology,* New York, 1952;

While all societies face the problem of allocating scarce resources, human effort, and organizational capacity among alternative ends, Western economics has evolved within the framework of large-scale industrial production and systems of marketing geared to this production. Thus, when the economist speaks of "credit," "capital," "scarcity," or "wealth" those concepts are linked to a body of experience based on the special case of Western economics.

An Eskimo hunter who distributes a newly caught seal in accordance with traditional patterns of allocation (from the moment the animal is killed every limb, every portion, is spoken for) may be said to establish "credit" among his kin folk. But this type of credit is so different, not only in degree but also in kind, to the credit that Western economists are wont to deal with, that lumping the two together and calling them manifestations of the same phenomenon obscures rather than enlightens.

Our hunter is securing himself and his family against want; now the giver, in due course he will become the recipient. But he has little choice, for custom dictates the form of distribution and the individuals who will share in his good fortune. Furthermore, if the credit he has established may in part be regarded as economic "credit," it is also very much social credit: his prestige as a hunter and his standing in the community have been enhanced. Perhaps one last word remains to be said. In simple societies of hunters, gatherers, and primitive agriculturalists, wealth generally takes the form of perishable commodities that must be allocated fairly rapidly or lose their value. Having hunted, the hunter must perforce distribute— he seldom can "save."

We shall return to the question of the economic organization of nonindustrial societies. The point to bear in mind is that even if it is valid to apply a general economic theory to both simple and complex, industrial and nonindustrial societies, the varieties in economic organization are such that it is imperative that the categories of economic analysis be applied with all due care. It is somewhat missing the mark to argue the general applicability of constructs derived

---

Raymond Firth, *Malay Fishermen: Their Peasant Economy*, Hamden, Conn., 1966; George Dalton, "Economic Theory and Primitive Society," *American Anthropologist*, 63: 1–25, 1961; Marshall D. Sahlins, "On the Sociology of Primitive Exchange," in Michael Banton, ed., *The Relevance of Models for Social Anthropology*, London, 1965; Edward E. LeClair, Jr. "Economic Theory and Economic Anthropology," *American Anthropologist*, 64: 1179–1202, 1962; Manning Nash, "The Organization of Economic Life," in Sol Tax, ed., *Horizons of Anthropology*, Chicago, 1964.

from Western economics; the danger is that these constructs tend to be freighted with implicit assumptions that may be irrelevant to economic reality at the level of less conplex societies.

What is desirable is an economic sensitivity allowing full scope to multiple avenues of change. Not unrelated to such a pluralistic approach is a question of no little moral importance. In the past, nations undergoing industrialization and massive economic change have often had to pay a heavy price in social dislocation and individual degradation for their initial economic successes. It is not necessary to espouse a romantic view of preindustrial society in order to recognize that economic change has generally been at the expense of some sectors of society, for the most part those least able to bear the cost. Some friction is inevitable as old forms give way to new, but it is indefensible to argue that whole generations of peasant and tribal folk must perforce be sacrificed in order to achieve developmental goals.

Both humanitarian and practical considerations—the two being by no means incompatible—demand developmental programs that respect cultural dignity and personal welfare. There is, for instance, a growing body of evidence that strongly suggests a relationship between malnutrition and mental retardation; apparently, malnourished children emerge from childhood with their intellectual capacities so thoroughly impaired that they may in many cases lack the talents to reach their full genetic potential. What physical misery and inadequate diet do to the body has long been recognized. Apparently, it is not only physical stature, but also mental stature, that is impaired.[6] These findings offer a new perspective to both the problems of transforming a disadvantaged peasantry into men able to find a place in the modern world and to various politico-economic rationalizations that would deprive a given generation in the supposed interests of the next. If curiosity, stamina, and energy are sapped at an early age—and never fully recovered—extreme deprivation will play havoc not only with the human resources of the present, but also those of the future.

Changes undertaken with the consent and partnership of the people can be expected to pay dividends in harmony and cooperation. While authority can impose change, by force if necessary, the mainsprings of economic behavior are rooted in attitudes and values that are deep seated and strongly resistant to purely external pressures. It is true that if sufficient force is applied most individuals will comply, but they will do so mechanically, by rote rather than

[6] Alan D. Berg, "Malnutrition and National Development," *Foreign Affairs*, Vol. 46, 1967, pp. 123–136.

through commitment and the expectation of material or psychological reward.

The ultimate goals of modernization, which for the average man can be summarized as better life chances for himself and his heirs, gain widespread support in most countries once the relationship between effort and goal is well enough understood. Contrary to popular assumptions current in the more affluent classes of both the developed and the underdeveloped world, no one is "naturally" happy in a condition of poverty and ignorance. Resignation there may be, but once people are made aware that a better life is possible *for them*, and that present efforts can contribute to future betterment, a major force is marshalled in the drive for modernization.

Underdeveloped countries may lack many of the features of economically developed lands, but they still differ substantially among themselves in degrees of development and forms of social and political organization. It is difficult to generalize for the underdeveloped world, and not much easier to generalize for many of its component countries. This is not to say that certain broad-gauge commonalities cannot be isolated, both in terms of regularities at the national scale and on the level of the cultures and part cultures that are the component parts of the state. For the purposes of this chapter attention will be chiefly directed to tribal societies and peasant cultures. The metropolitan sectors of society—those more directly associated with urban phenomena and the national culture per se—will be only touched upon. Elaboration is reserved for later chapters.

ECONOMICS AND TRIBAL LIFE

While there are considerable differences among tribal societies, such societies are everywhere integrated according to a limited set of principles. Subsistence may be based on hunting or gathering, pastoralism, or simple forms of agriculture. Regardless of how livelihood is obtained, technology is universally simple, skills tend to be generalized (there is little division of labor), and the productive capacities of the individual are restricted. Even in cases where levels of productivity are fairly high, difficulties of transportation and storage and the general absence of markets (both in the specific sense of trading centers and the more generalized meaning of outlets for production) limit the use to which surpluses may be put. A fairly general, though not universal, feature of such societies in times of plenty is the display and destruction of goods that cannot be consumed at the moment or kept for the future.[7]

Economically, the temporal horizon of tribesmen is circumscribed, limited for the most part to the yearly round of the agricultural season or the periodicity of game herds. With little to fall back upon in times of need, survival depends to a great extent on institutionalized forms of exchange, sharing, and distribution. Economies with such little leeway cannot afford major discriminations in wealth and fortune; as previously noted, the lucky hunter must share with the empty handed, the good crops of some must compensate for the poor harvests of others. The transactional principles governing the distribution of material goods in such societies have been summarized by Dalton as follows:

The integrative patterns that do exist widely in primitive economy are (1) reciprocity, that is material gift and counter gift-giving induced by social obligation and derived, typically, from kinship . . . . and (2) redistribution, the channeling upwards of goods and services to socially determined allocative centers (usually king, chief, or priest), who then redistribute either to their subordinates at large by providing community services, or in specific allotments to individuals in accordance with their political, religious, or military status.[8]

Malinowski—writing from a more limited perspective—reached much the same conclusion when he observed that "the chief on the one hand has the power to accumulate agricultural produce and to control the livestock and palms of the district, while on the other hand, he is the one who has both the right and duty to use this accumulated wealth effectively."[9]

[7] The most flamboyant of these manifestations is the "potlatch" custom of the Kwakiutl of the northwest coast of North America. On the Kwakiutl and their rather complex social and economic behavior, see Helen Codere, *Fighting With Property*, New York, 1951, and Philip Drucker, *Cultures of the North Pacific*, San Francisco, 1965. Potlatch type phenomena have been recorded from other regions of the globe, especially Melanesia. See also Bronislaw Malinowski, *The Argonauts of the Western Pacific*, London, 1922, for a classic description of the exchange, display, and wasting of goods.

[8] George Dalton, "Economic Theory and Primitive Society," *American Anthropologist*, Vol. 63, No. 1, 1961, p. 9.

[9] Bronislaw Malinowski, *Coral Gardens and Their Magic*, Vol. 1, London, 1934, p. 47. Although written almost half a century ago, Marcel Mauss' *Essai sur le don, forme archaïque de l'échange* (1925), translated by Ian Cunnison as *The Gift, Forms and Functions of Exchange in Archaic Societies*, Glencoe, Ill., 1954, is still perhaps the most erudite examination of primitive exchange. For a more recent discussion, see M. D. Sahlins, "On the Sociology of Primitive Exchange," in Michael Banton, ed., *The Relevance of Models for Social Anthropology*, London, 1965, pp. 139–236.

Another characteristic of primitive economic activity is the degree
to which it is integrated with the whole fabric of social life. Economic
phenomena interface with the moral, religious, mythological, and
juridical dimensions of tribal life. Magic and religion are interwoven
into productive techniques and rules of allocation, while major social
events and critical economic activities are interdependent: the annual
hunt, the harvest season, and the yearly salmon run are almost surely
to be high points in both the social and economic calendar. In much
the same way, dyadic social relations generally entail some economic
involvement. It is therefore difficult for the outsider to factor out
pure economic pursuits, for the reality he is faced with is a series of
defined obligations, with some economic tangent, backed by all the
sanctions at the disposal of society. While some transactional patterns
may link a number of discrete tribal groups—as Malinowski so
vividly recorded in his pioneer studies of the Trobriand Islands—
such relationships also tend to be fixed by custom rather than by
strictly economic dictates.[10]

It would be quite wrong, however, to assume that primitive man
is unaware or unconcerned with the practical problems of making a
living. In fact, the forms of organization that we have outlined have
the effect of securing an element of predictability in the tasks of
subsistence. There is no reason to assume that because the instru-
mentals of survival are hedged about by magic and religion there is
some failure to recognize cause and effect. Ritual does not plant the
corn nor havest it; the game animals are not brought low by incanta-
tions. No substitute exists for the effort and skill of the farmer or the
cunning of the huntsman. What religion does provide is a degree of
support and assurance, a most valuable ingredient for a people re-
siding at the edge of subsistence. Broadly speaking, all customary behavior is a pledge that the present will resemble the past and the
future will resemble the present.[11]

[10] Apart from contributions already cited, see also, Malinowski, "Kula: The
Circulating Exchange of Valuables in the Archipelagoes of Eastern New
Guinea," *Man*, No. 51, 1920, pp. 97–105.

[11] Where custom and religion are binding forces, resistance to change may
be strong. Also it has been argued that rituals create the very anxieties they
purport to assuage. See A. R. Radcliffe-Brown, *Structure and Function in
Primitive Society*, London, 1961, pp. 148–149, 174–175.

THE TRANSFORMATION OF TRIBAL LIFE

Simple societies of this type constitute almost totally closed systems, logical in themselves, but with little relation to, or understanding of, the world of more complex societies. The dangers in such a situation is that more sophisticated groups will penetrate the isolation of simple societies and attempt to apply totally alien concepts, economic and otherwise. Tribal-type structures are in the main much more "brittle" than established peasantries, for they lack experience in accommodating to powerful external cultural influences. Thus, while peasant groups may bend under pressure, tribal groups are generally faced with what amounts to a choice between hopeless resistance and total cultural capitulation.

Simple societies have always been vulnerable and, in fact, one can read human history since the advent of cities and kingdoms as a progressive subjugation of tribal folk by the forces of metropolitan society. In contemporary times, though, the pace of penetration has quickened and at the same time the cultural distance separating complex from simple societies has grown. Measured in terms of cultural dislocation, it must be admitted that for tribesmen as a whole the price of contact with more advanced people has come high. The anthropological record is quite clear: culture clash is a reality that manifests itself in terms of cultural malaise, the incapacity of people who have been stripped of social and emotional security to carry on a meaningful existence. The old ways, the traditional solutions, are found to be inapplicable, the new incomprehensible.

Yet, paradoxically, the values of tribal life, while superficially very different from those of modern society, are not necessarily incompatible with technological and economic advancement. Adaptation is easier for peasant societies than for tribal ones, but very often, adaptation takes the form of a passive holding action, a resignation born of long experience in subordination. At least some tribal societies carry within them the potential for a more meaningful transformation. The very autonomy of tribal groups assures an element of indigenous leadership and the presence of avenues for communal action. These components do not in themselves assure innovation, but they do provide a framework for internally directed change.

One of Margaret Mead's more recent anthropological contributions is a study of change and leadership in a simple Admiralty Islands society. The group in question, the Manus, experienced during the Second World War the effects of a massive American military presence. Military occupation was not designed as an exercise in progressive culture change, but the benign conditions under which cultural alternatives were presented so transformed the fabric of native culture that it is fair to speak of a veritable quantum jump in expectations, attitudes, and organizational forms. In Mead's words:

A people who, under the old complex system of aid and ceremonial, had been able to build only two or three houses a year, now built sixty houses in a little over two months. The new villages were designed to express the new concepts. Every house had the same dimensions and all had separate rooms for separate purposes. There was a central square in which meetings were to be held. Skeleton versions of "docks," "customs," "hostels," "hospitals," "schools," and "banks" were set up. The old practices were examined, and new rules were made about the amount of expenditure that was appropriate for a wedding and a funeral. Individual economic responsibility was introduced, together with communitywide use of unused lands and community provision for widows and orphans and the sick. A common treasury was established, and into this went money made during the war, to be drawn upon for the common good of the entire movement . . . By 1949, a neolithic society . . . (had been transformed) into a very crude but systematic version of a mid-twentieth century society.[12]

Obviously, something more was involved than an overwhelming number of American servicemen. The Admiralty Islands have a long tradition of nativistic movements known as cargo cults. These cults, although clearly related to European contact and colonizations, are essentially symbolic and religious, while what occurred in Manus society was an attempt to bring about a transformation in terms of the real aspects of modern culture. Again, to quote Mead, people "make definite plans for the incorporation of European features of housing, dress, and manners, and they make specific demands for schooling."[13] Indubitably, this shift in cultural orientation was much facilitated by the decent conduct of American soldiers. The average American reacted to the Manus "not as natives to be kept in their place, or as future plantation workers, or even as members of another race, but simply as amusing and competent companions."[14] The Manus, for their part, perceived the Americans as "beautifully

[12] Margaret Mead, *Continuities in Cultural Evolution*. New Haven, Conn., 1964, p. 211. See also Mead's monograph on Manus cultural transformation, *New Lives for Old, Cultural Transformation-Manus, 1928–1953*, New York, 1956.

[13] Mead, *op. cit.*, p. 196.

[14] Mead, *Continuities. . . . op. cit.*, p. 207.

equipped technically, and they connected this high level of technology with a different kind of social organization."[15]

Two other factors help to account for the success of Manus transformation. One of these, a tradition of local leadership that permits men of superior qualities to play innovative roles, has already been alluded to. This is combined in Manus culture with a generally high evaluation of personal initiative and independence. McClelland observes that the catalytic influence of wartime contact with the United States Armed Forces must be understood as working on well-prepared ground. In 1930 Mead had noted that the Munus lived in platform houses set up on poles over the sea.

It was therefore easy for young children to fall off into the sea and drown. The Manus had responded to this Toynbeean "challenge" by requiring that their children learn to swim and take care of themselves in the water quite early. In fact, they built them small canoes and literally taught them to "paddle their own canoes" at a very early age. Does it seem too far-fetched to assume that we have evidence for a linkage here between . . . the early independence training . . . and rapid technological development once contact with superior knowledge is made?[16]

The adult, trained in youth to exercise initiative and independence will hardly change his orientation later in life. We make no claim that Manus represents a "typical" primitive society, for surely such societies encompass a wide range of behavioral forms and attitudes. It remains true, however, that even the simplest cultures can carry within them the seeds of revolutionary change.

Economic life in peasant communities

In contrast to tribal-type societies, peasant communities are to some degree linked to more complex organizational structures, national or regional in scope, and directed from urban power centers.

[15] *Ibid.*, p. 206.

[16] David C. McClelland, "Some Social Consequences of Achievement Motivation," *Nebraska Symposium on Motivation*, edited by Marshall R. Jones, Lincoln, Nebraska, 1955, p. 59. In recent years, development economists have focused more attention on the question of value orientations and motivations for change. See, for example, T. R. Brannen and Frank X. Hodgson, *Overseas Management*, New York, 1965; and E. E. Hagen, *On the Theory of Social Change*, Homewood, Ill., 1962.

But insofar as the local web of interpersonal relations in concerned, the peasantry have in common a number of features with tribal society. Thus, customary patterns of aid and cooperation, distribution and allocation, are deep-rooted in peasant life. Kinship, whether geared to the nuclear family or to more extended "stem" forms, counts for much as a principle of social structure, not excluding the economic sphere, while in many cases substantial effort is directed to meeting the material demands of religious observance and social position. The extent to which culturally defined obligations can structure social and economic life is illustrated in the case of the Indian peasants of Panajachel in Western Guatemala. The inhabitants of this village trade the produce of their rich truck gardens and coffee groves with the national capital and other urban centers. With the proceeds of trade, Panajacheleños purchase articles and manufactured goods that are not produced in the community. At the same time, a society of some eight hundred individuals must allocate surpluses to support a total of fifty-two offices in the indigenous (as distinct from the national) politico-religious hierarchy. These offices are ranked in increasing prestige and commensurate expense, and every man in his time can hope or, rather, is expected to work his way up the organizational ladder. What ceremonialism, public and private, secular and religious, entails in terms of relative expenditure can be gauged by the importance of alcohol in the family budgets. This ingredient, essential in virtually all ceremonial activities, represents "about a fourth of that spent on clothing, it is more than that of any item of food excepting corn and meat; and is almost as much as that spent on all tools and household utensils and supplies."[17] This is not meant to imply that such levels of ceremonial expenditure are typical for all peasant societies, although peasants, not unlike tribesmen, do tend to establish priorities and earmark surpluses in a manner likely to puzzle economists.

As a rule, peasant productivity is low, especially in terms of output per worker, which of course does not preclude expenditure on non-subsistence activities. Low levels of productivity are for the most part a consequence of low levels of technology and the inefficient disposal of human resources. Technical backwardness is in turn partly responsible for the poverty, distrust, and anxiety that are so much part of the peasant scene in many regions of the world. Yet, this climate of physical and psychological insecurity cannot all be accounted for by narrow economic margins. Other factors enter the

[17] Sol Tax, *Penny Capitalism: A Guatemalan Indian Economy*, Chicago, 1963, p. 117.

equation. The potential for higher productivity and a better standard of living may be present in some peasant societies even without major changes of a technological nature. But the potential can remain unrealized if peasants fear that those in positions of power and authority will deprive them of increments resulting from greater labor and effort. While the situation is obviously not the same everywhere, peasants may have good historical reasons to fear that production much above the subsistence level ultimately will be siphoned off in the form of higher taxes, feudal-type dues, law suits, and similar other calls on surpluses. Regardless of whether the peasant evaluates the contemporary situation correctly, attitudes born of such expectations become woven into the fabric of peasant life and action and guide economic behavior.

Peasant societies react to a hard environment in different, and sometimes diametrically opposed, ways. Patterns of rapid and conspicuous consumption like those described by Sol Tax for Panajachel may be founded on the philosophy that the pleasures of today cannot be taken away tomorrow, that it is better to spend while the opportunity presents itself. Other groups insist on frugality as the best hope for security. The Basseri of South Persia evidence "an almost obsessive desire to postpone every incident of consumption—to let each lamb gain weight one more day, or week, or season, to have one more lamb from an old sheep, to make a worn-out pair of shoes last till the next market town, or till arrival in the summer area, or till next spring equinox (the Persian New Year, when it is customary to put on new clothes)."[18]

ECONOMIC CHANGE AND THE CONCEPT OF A LIMITED GOOD

Business and interpersonal relations conducted within the framework of a small community can best be understood as a series of individual negotiations and adjustments. Relationships are therefore subject to a degree of mutual accomodation and codes of national

[18] Fredrik Barth, "Capital, Investment and the Social Structure of a Pastoral Nomad Group in South Persia," in Raymond Firth and B. S. Yamey, eds., *Capital, Saving and Credit in Peasant Societies*, Chicago, 1963, p. 79. While the Basseri are pastoralists, and may thus be said to be somewhat atypical, their frugal ways are not at all unlike that of many settled peasant communities.

interpersonal ethics are either discarded or little heeded. Adjustment is not always easy, for there may lurk the suspicion that for someone to win, someone else must lose, that each individual is motivated by personal interest or the interest of family, caste, or similar entity. Those in positions of influence and leadership, whether local men or outsiders, are typically distrusted and envied. In the words of a villager from Northern India:

When we see a police constable or deputy's assistant in the village we know that someone is going to be threatened and will have to part with some of his money. Who are the men who own watches and live in brick houses? Not one of us here thinks that he can afford a watch, it is in the luxury class. But the minor officials all own watches. . . . Who pays for this? We do![19]

While not all peasants live in grinding poverty, deprivation has been, and in many cases continues to be a common enough phenomenon to have influenced the formation of what George Foster has called "the image of the limited good,"[20] a world view based on the assumption that the good things of life, and sometimes even the minima for living, are fixed in quantity. According to Foster:

peasants view their social, economic, and natural universes—their total environment—as one in which all the desired things in life such as land, wealth, health, friendship and love, manliness and honor, respect and status, power and influence, security and safety, *exist in finite quantity* and *are always in short supply*, as far as the peasant is concerned. Not only do these and all other "good things" exist in finite and limited quantities, but in addition *there is no way directly within the peasant power to increase the available quantities.*[21]

Foster is careful to disclaim universality for his model. There is strong evidence, though, that something akin to what Foster describes for the peasants of Tzintzuntzan is deeply entrenched in the

[19] William and Charlotte Wiser, *Behind Mud Walls, 1930–1960*, Berkeley and Los Angeles, 1963. On factionalism, rivalry, distrust, and envy in peasant societies, see George M. Foster, "Interpersonal Relations in a Peasant Society," *Human Organization*, 1960–1961, Vol. 19, No. 4, pp. 174–178, and in the same issue, "Comments and Rejoinder" by Oscar Lewis, Julian Pitt-Rivers, and George M. Foster.

[20] George M. Foster, "Peasant Society and the Image of the Limited Good," *American Anthropologist*, 1965, Vol. 67, No. 2, pp. 293–315.

[21] Ibid., p. 296. For two critiques of Foster's model, see Steven Piker, "The Image of the Limited Good: Comments on an Exercise in Description and Interpretation," *American Anthropologist*, 1966, Vol. 68, No. 5, pp. 1202–1211, and, same issue, John G. Kennedy, "Peasant Society and the Image of the Limited Good: A Critique," pp. 1212–1225.

European peasant ethos. Again and again, we encounter a great concern for fair shares, a belief that the natural state of man is to be found in the equal distribution of goods or the holding of all property in common. John Ball, leader and spokesman of the English Peasants' Revolt of 1381, is said to have preached to the assembled peasants on a text which was then a traditional proverb and has remained famous to this day:

> When Adam delved and Eve span
> Who was then a gentleman?[22]

Another medieval sermon pictures the plight of the poor peasant in contrast to the opulence of the rich.

O just God, mightly judge, the game was not fairly divided between them and us. Their satiety was our famine; their merriment was our wretchedness; their jousts and tournaments were our torments.[23]

The theme of equality is not limited to medieval peasants' revolts. In the nineteenth century, a Sicilian peasant woman echoed the ideas of the fourteenth century Englishman.

We want everybody to work, as we work. There should no longer be either rich or poor. All should have bread for themselves and their children. We should all be equal.[24]

Clearly, much more is involved in peasant-type revolts than a perception of the universe limited in the desiderata of life. One must take into consideration oppressive conditions and the millenary expectations of a grand redistribution of wealth that is to follow the downfall of the rich and mighty. But there is nothing inconsistent in these other aspects of peasant movements of rebellion with the image of a static economy. The powerful have taken more than their due, and the situation should be put to rights. One cannot escape the impression that for the peasant the wealth of some automatically spells the poverty of others.

It is not alone the rich and the powerful—generally speaking, members of nonpeasant directing classes—who are singled out for resentment, suspicion, and envy. Only occasionally have peasants dared to challenge in open revolt those normally enjoying a monopoly of

[22] Norman Cohn, *The Pursuit of the Millenium*, New York, 1961, p. 211.
[23] *Ibid.*, p. 214.
[24] E. J. Hobsbawm, *Primitive Rebels: Studies in Archaic Forms of Social Movement in the Nineteenth and Twentieth Centuries*, New York, 1963, cited in Joel M. Halpern, *The Changing Village Community*, Englewood Cliffs, N.J., 1967, p. 27.

power. Much more typical, and much more corrosive, is resentment turned inward against other members of the peasant group. No great wealth is necessary to qualify for ill feeling; a farmer's new hoe or a housewife's new utensil might, in fact, prove quite sufficient to occasion gossip and generate friction. The least one can say is that in most peasant societies individual success is hardly calculated to receive the plaudits of one's neighbors.

With poverty a normative condition and an ethos geared to the assumption that the individual cannot do much to change his condition, it is hard for the peasant to escape the notion that fate, rather than effort, dictates the ways of men. It is almost as if life were a trickster, giving and taking at random, but mostly taking.

Today you think you are going at least to have enough to eat, and all of a sudden something happens. Someone steals your donkey—or God takes him away; a child becomes ill; your wheat doesn't get that last needed drop of rain; a daughter needs a dowry for her marriage. There is always something that keeps you down and in desperate circumstances.[25]

In truth, too often there is little that the peasant can do to change his lot, for it is not simply a peasant myth that the small man lacks the power to alter his destiny. But regardless of whether in fact the peasant's welfare lies outside his control, the belief that it does so is sufficient to make the prophecy self-fulfilling. For the peasant, wisdom lies in taking life as it comes.

> You who are hurried,
> Stay and accept your censure,
> Daily bread comes from God,
> It is not for you to concern yourself.[26]

As Banfield observes, attitudes of this type influence economic behavior.

One who lives in so capricious a world is not likely to save and invest in the expectation of ultimate gain. In politics, too, it must have an effect. Where everything depends upon luck or Divine intervention, there is no point in community action. The community, like the individual, may hope and pray, but it is not likely to take its destiny into its own hands.[27]

[25] Joseph Lopreato, *Peasants No More: Social Class and Social Change in an Underdeveloped Society*, San Francisco, 1967, p. 245.

[26] Pierre Bourdieu, "The Attitude of the Algerian Peasant Towards Time," *Mediterranean Countrymen*, Julian Pitt-Rivers, ed., Paris and La Haye, 1963, p. 58.

[27] Edward C. Banfield, *The Moral Basis of a Backward Society*, New York, 1967, p. 97.

It is only fair to point out that Banfield is writing of one of the most downtrodden peasantries in the world, the villagers of southern Italy.[28] Where the economic base is less precarious, and social conditions permit a degree of initiative, opportunities do exist for community action. For the most part, the peasants of northern and western Europe, and increasingly, those of some Balkan and central European regions, do not regard themselves as the playthings of fate. But these are peasants who form part of economically and politically advanced states, or who at least have witnessed the reality of change and modernization.[29] To be frank, a sense of progress—a recognition that change is possible and that alternatives offering a better life are, or can be made, available—is not too often encountered as a feature of peasant society in the underdeveloped world. In many cases, leadership functions have for so long been monopolized by out-group individuals and institutions that even the concept of autonomy of action is alien.

PEASANTS, SOCIAL CLASS, AND NATIONAL ADVANCEMENT

The quality of peasant poverty warrants a final comment. Tribesmen are "poor" in the sense that their material resources are limited and that they generally lack much in the way of cash (or commodities with market value) for the purchase of goods and products outside customary channels of barter and exchange. But tribesmen live, or have lived until recently, in self-contained worlds offering few opportunities for a comparative evaluation of wealth. Within the tribal spectrum, wealth differences do not begin to approach the gulf that separates peasant from elite in traditional society. Peasants,

[28] Perhaps the classic statement of southern Italian peasant misery and desperation—*la miseria*—is Carlo Levi's social novel, *Christ Stopped at Eboli*, New York, 1946. Although the novel is based on observations made in the middle nineteen-thirties, the conditions depicted remained essentially unchanged until very recent times.

[29] See, for example, Robert T. Anderson and Barbara Gallatin Anderson, *The Vanishing Village, A Danish Maritime Community*, Seattle, 1964; Joel M. Halpern, *Social and Cultural Change in a Serbian Village*, New Haven, Conn., 1956; Laurence Wylie, *Village in the Vaucluse*, New York, 1964; E. W. Martin, *The Shearers and the Shorn, A Study of Life in a Devon Community*, London, 1965.

on the other hand, operate in a context where wealth and power are monopolized by local and national upper classes. The poverty of the peasant is therefore more pernicious, much more degrading. It is associated with the lower orders of society, those who by necessity must work the soil. There is nothing comparable in tribal society to the degredation associated with manual farm labor in traditional societies.

It is obvious, therefore, that in order to achieve modernization, not only peasant attitudes must change, but equally important changes must occur in the society as a whole. Peasants must be made to feel that they have a stake in national institutions; that any contributions they make will in some way benefit their lives; that initiative and effort will be rewarded rather than suppressed. These are not changes that peasants can undertake by themselves. A change in attitudes must either evolve in the process of induced economic change or, given the nature of the current political and social situation over much of the underdeveloped world, it is likely to be forged in the fires of violent revolution.

In most underdeveloped countries, the middle and upper classes, while clearly separate from the peasantry with respect to education, style of life, and the capacity to influence and control events, nevertheless share with them significant attributes in values and the modalities of interpersonal relations. It is not peasants alone who structure interpersonal relations according to what has been termed the principle of "personalism."[30] Typically, all sectors of society allocate loyalty, effort, and concern on the basis of previously established ties, usually family membership, but not excluding such links as ethnic group, religious community, locality of origin, and other ascribed bonds. It is perfectly true that criteria of this type influence action and behavior in all societies, not excluding economically developed ones. The difference is therefore relative, but the difference nevertheless counts a great deal. In traditional societies it appears that little concern is felt for those outside the reference group and that in practice the interests of organizational structures that do not affect one directly are subordinated to personal gain, group interests, or perhaps simply ignored.

Hauser, writing of conditions prevalent in South and Southeast Asia—but which are certainly not restricted to the area—is of the opinion that

The atomistic behaviorisms which, perhaps, have the greatest retarding

[30] William F. Whyte and Allan Holmberg, "Human Problems of U.S. Enterprise in Latin America," *Human Organization*, Vol. 15, No. 3, 1956, p. 3.

influence on economic development include: 1) the comparative lack of discipline, regularity, and regimentation as they affect labor force activity; 2) the tendency to "mind one's own business" to a point where obligation and responsibility to others is almost completely ignored; 3) the insecurity of physical property as evidenced by widespread theft and "decoity"; 4) the emphasis on personal rather than organizational practice; and 5) the general lack of national or organizational consciousness or imagery.[31]

This behavioral and attitudinal complex, so reminiscent of certain aspects of the peasant ethos, is obviously highly detrimental to the proper functioning of large organizational structures, be they political or economic, national or private. And yet it is perfectly true that much in the same way as peasants desire material improvement—better crops, better housing, a more equitable division of the fruits of their labor—the societies of the underdeveloped world crave the benefits of modernization. The problem is that traditional attitudes and behaviorisms persist at the same time that changes are not only desired, but desired in a great hurry. At all levels of society, from ministerial office to peasant's hut, there is a growing awareness that something is being lost, for like the medieval preacher who claimed that the game was not fairly divided, the inhabitants of the poor nations are beginning to contrast their poverty to the affluence of the developed world. A desire for change is in the air, but beneath all the turmoil, all the dissatisfaction, "there is a vast inertia, a great ocean of people and tradition, slow to respond to the storm at the surface."[32] Given the cultural obstacles to technological change and modernization, it is not surprising that one writer is "tempted . . . to question the wisdom and even sometimes the safety" of engaging in programs of rapid transformation. "The whole thing suggests to me an attempt to present the Bonneville Power System to St. Thomas Aquinas." Yet, he is sure "that there is no practical use in asking whether this is good or safe. These questions are not only very complicated, but also irrelevant."[33]

The fact remains, though, that modernization cannot proceed, has no chance of success, unless it is matched by concomitant shifts in attitudes and values. There must be a readiness to take risks inherent in operating outside the groove of tradition. If peasants are

[31] Phillip M. Hauser, "Cultural and Physical Obstacles to Economic Development in the Less Delevoped Areas," *Human Organization*, Vol. 18, No. 2, 1959, p. 82.

[32] Francis E. Dart, "The Rub of Cultures," *Education and the Development of Nations*, John W. Hanson and Cole S. Brembeck, eds., New York, 1966, p. 93.

[33] *Ibid.*, p. 94.

asked to venture their future on new crops and new marketing arrangements, the middle and upper classes must be pressed to make comparable shifts. As a case in point, it is not only peasants that hide harvests and deny wealth; the normal middle class attitude in many countries is that only the simple minded pay income taxes willingly.[34]

Taking into consideration all the factors we have presented, one must conclude that the modernization of traditional society demands change at many levels. The betterment of the peasantry, important though this is, represents but one aspect of a series of parallel shifts encompassing the whole fabric of national life. Peasant attitudes and peasant poverty are as much a product of the peasant's place in the nation as of any limitations in technology. Without doubt it is harder to program change for a whole country than to introduce modernization to a small self-contained tribal group, and it would appear that at times the problem is much more than one of scale.

It is pertinent also to keep an eye on history, to remember that in the past the good life for some has been at the expense of the many. The modern analog is a superficial modernization that touches only some sectors of society, a modernization that is strictly material and strictly circumscribed. Meaningful, genuine change demands that all sectors of society not only recognize their own stake in modernization but manifest a willingness to do all in their power to contribute to the tasks of modernization. As it has been so aptly put by Erich Fromm, the members of a society "must acquire the kind of character which makes them *want* to act in the way they *have* to act as members of the society or of a special class within it. They have to *desire* what objectively is necessary for them to do."[35] In the last analysis, the technologies and organizational forms of the developed lands, their science and accumulated experience, their loans, grants and good intentions, will count for nought unless they are grafted to a home-grown willingness to experiment and innovate. One can perhaps generalize for traditional societies what has been written to apply to the problem of change in agricultural practices.

Introducing a new factor of production would mean not only breaking with the past but coping with a problem, because the production possi-

[34] In the past, especially in former colonial areas, it was fair game not to cooperate with structures operating at the national level. Although political reality has changed, a similar reordering of social attitudes has seldom taken place.

[35] Erich Fromm, "Individual and Social Origins of Neurosis," *Personality in Nature, Society, and Culture*, Clyde Kluckhohn and Henry R. Murray, eds., New York, 1953, p. 517.

bilities of the new factor will be subject to risks and uncertainties as yet unknown. It is therefore not sufficient merely to adopt the new factors and reap the larger return; learning from experience what new risks and uncertainties are inherent in these factors is also entailed.[36]

BIBLIOGRAPHY

Dalton, George (ed.), *Tribal and Peasant Economies: Readings in Economic Anthropology*, New York, 1967.

Foster, George M., *Culture and Conquest: America's Spanish Heritage*, Chicago, 1960.

Foster, George M., *Traditional Cultures: The Impact of Technological Change*, New York, 1962.

Goodenough, Ward H., *Cooperation in Change: An Anthropological Approach to Community Development*, New York, 1966.

Harding, Thomas G., *Voyagers of the Vitiaz Straits: A Study of a New Guinea Trade System*, Seattle, 1967.

Lewis, Oscar, *Five Families: Mexican Case Studies in the Culture of Poverty*, New York, 1962.

Nash, Manning, *Machine Age Maya*, American Anthropological Association, Memoir 87, Vol. 60, No. 2, Part 2, April 1958.

Richards, Audrey I. (ed.), *Economic Development and Tribal Change*, Cambridge, Mass., n.d.

Southall, A. (ed.), *Social Change in Modern Africa*, London, 1961.

UNESCO, *Social Implications of Industrialization and Urbanization in Africa South of the Sahara*, Paris, 1956.

Spicer, E. H. (ed.), *Human Problems in Technological Change*, New York, 1966.

van den Berghe, Pierre L. (ed.), *Africa: Social Problems of Change and Conflict*, San Francisco, 1965.

Wagley, Charles, *Amazon Town*, New York, 1964.

Watson, W., *Tribal Cohesion in a Money Economy*, Manchester, 1958.

Wolf, Eric, *Sons of the Shaking Earth*, Chicago, 1962.

Yang, C. K., *Chinese Communist Society: The Family and the Village*, Cambridge, Mass., 1959.

[36] Theodore W. Schultz. *Transforming Traditional Agriculture*, New Haven, Conn., 1964, p. 32.

III

❋

Agriculture and Technological Change

THE ECOLOGY OF TECHNOLOGICAL TRANSFER

Agricultural techniques, like other forms of technology, are in origin adaptations to particular environmental and cultural situations. As such, the successful diffusion of agriculture entails both a recognition of ecological potentials and limitations and an understanding of the cultural and social context associated with a particular form of agricultural practice. Western agricultural concepts often reflect the conditions of the North Temperate Zone where these ideas evolved. To those brought up in a given technological tradition it is often difficult to distinguish between those elements of tool-using behavior which have near-universal validity and the ones that are products of a specific setting.

Considering technology in terms of its problem-solving character, we can distinguish between the historical accumulation of techniques (which may or may not have relevance to other areas) and those methods of enquiry and empirical verification that have evolved as a concomitant of these techniques.

Certainly, the concepts of ecology are as much a product of Western agricultural experience as are specific agricultural implements or practices. Thus, when we speak of the lack of relevance of certain parts of Western agricultural technology to the agricultural problems of underdeveloped areas, it should be clear that reference is made to specific techniques rather than to the broader scope and method of Western science and technology.

The problem of ecological adaptation is not new. The history of domestication records numerous instances of the adaptation of plants and animals to new locations. The spread of agriculture and husbandry from its focus of origin in the Near East to first and Mediterranean littoral and later the temperate areas of Central and Northern Europe constitutes one of the best documented cases of progressive adaptation. In this process adjustments were necessary in the total agricultural complex: the conscious selection of seeds and animals, the adaptation of tools, and the adjustment to new seasonal and climatic requirements. Similarly, one may cite the transformation of rice from a highland grain crop to a wet land staple in monsoon Asia, a change that entailed a whole range of technological developments, including such complex techniques as irrigation, terracing, and the use of primary nurseries.

Even the diffusion of simple agricultural technology requires an adjustment either in the technology itself or in the recipient culture. The spade, for instance, presupposes a sturdily-shod work force. The European-introduced spade has never superseded the native digging stick, the *coa*, in some areas of Middle America even after three hundred years of cultural contact. The *coa*, constructed with a built-in platform, allows the barefooted agriculturalist to apply the weight of his body in working the soil. While seldom as efficient as the spade, the *coa* is better integrated with the traditional culture. For basically similar reasons, the spade has not displaced traditional implements in many other regions.

HOE CULTIVATION

Hoe cultivation is still extensively practiced throughout the world. There are a variety of factors that explain the persistence of this technique in the face of more sophisticated approaches. Historically, the lack of appropriate domesticated animals, such as occurred in pre-Columbian America, has meant that man constituted the sole source of motive power for working the land. In certain parts of Africa it has proved impossible to introduce draft animals because of the tsetse fly and other disease carriers. While mechanization of agriculture can overcome most of these limitations, other ecological factors (such as the properties of the soil) may restrict the use of modern technology. The notable lack of success of the Tanganyika groundnut scheme can be attributed to the failure of Western specialists to recognize the limits of specific technological practices. Deep plowing by heavy machinery disturbed the composition of the soil and restructured it into a hard, smooth surface lacking aeration. According to Stamp:

Although the barefoot of the African cultivator may tread with impunity on the soil, a caterpillar tractor has the same effect as a road roller and consolidates the surface into a hard macadam layer. . . . The angular quartz grains (harder than any steel) embedded in a clay matrix seemed to have acted just like diamond dust in a circular iron wheel; they rasped the steel discs of a plow in an incredibly short time.[1]

At a more elementary level, the introduction of draft animals requires adjustments in patterns of cultivation and, consequently, changes in cultural perspectives. In many regions of hoe cultivation, slash-and-burn agriculture is the prevailing form. Typically, the branches from trees and bushes are cut and piled on the ground to dry. When properly timed before the rains, the burning of the accumulated vegetation provides nutriment to the soil. Obviously, a precondition of plow cultivation is the removal of stumps and roots; but in slash-and-burn agriculture these provide an element of protection against soil erosion. This protection may be lost if the Western ideal of a cleared field—the product of temperate zone experience— is heedlessly resorted to.

The hoe cultivator has the discretion of selecting the better soils within the limits of his field and rejecting other patches as unfit for further processing. On the other hand, the western cultivator with draft animal or mechanized plow is forced to be less discriminating in working a large and regular area. Variations in soil fertility are evened out with fertilizers and other techniques.[2]

[1] Dudley Stamp, *Africa: A Study in Tropical Development*, New York, 1953, p. 96.
[2] W. Allan, *The African Husbandman*, Edinburgh, 1965, pp. 96–97.

Traditional social structure and
slash-and-burn agriculture

Slash-and-burn requires large reserves of land in order to provide for a lengthy regenerative cycle. Throughout much of the world, population pressures are forcing land into recultivation before it has regained fertility. This leads to a spiral of successively poorer crops and rapid soil erosion.

Population pressures alone dictate a shift from the hoe to more sophisticated forms of cultivation. This cannot be achieved successfully without developing techniques for the maintenance and protection of the soil. Even so, in many marginal areas it may be advantageous to develop alternate forms of cultivation that are better related to the ecological conditions. For example, arboreal cultivation —cacao, palm oil, rubber, and so on—protects the soil against tropical heat and heavy rains.

Land use is integrally related to the social structure of the community. Slash-and-burn is usually associated with communal forms of land ownership. The group, whether lineage, tribe, or village, assigns to the individual cultivator the use-rights of certain plots of land. The allocation of these rights is controlled by traditional authorities vested with powers having the force of law. Communal ownership does not mean that the individual cultivator lacks fair claim to the land he uses and the produce therefrom. On the contrary, membership in the group guarantees use-right to a portion of the communal holdings.

In the context of traditional society and agriculture this system has been functional and flexible. Given the level of technology, a system of shifting agriculture is clearly compatible with periodic division of the land. Up to the present, this flexibility has withstood the impact of substantial outmigration of workers to urban areas and other places of monetary employment. In such cases the land is divided among the remaining population while the rights of those absent are preserved for their return. In areas of acute land shortage the opportunities of outside employment may well be a factor in preserving traditional structures by relieving pressures on the land. It is questionable whether under these conditions a more individualized system of tenure would have allowed for as full a use of available land resources.

Communal ownership with individual use-rights is, however,

clearly incompatible with modern agronomy. Crop rotation, fertilization, and mechanization involve a long term commitment to the care and nurture of the soil. Experience has shown, however, that private property in fee simply may not be the solution to this dilemma. Often the rigid application of Western property concepts has led to a loss of land by indigenous cultivators and the creation of a disinherited rural proletariat. In other areas, such as Japan, small peasant holdings have proved to be compatible with modernization and not destructive of peasant values. It should be noted, however, that this condition in Japanese agriculture was to a large extent the result of a planned program of land reform. Conversely, the periodic and ill-conceived attempts to introduce fee simple among reservation Indians in the United States has been disastrous, with few exceptions. To a people for whom tribal identity and communal ownership were inseparable, the division of land was the opening wedge for the alienation of the land and rapid social disintegration. The Western rituals of land transference were interpreted by the Indians as granting a use-right and not as a permanent abrogation of traditional rights.

This pattern has been replicated wherever European peoples have come into contact with indigenous societies. In areas of shifting cultivation, what were "empty lands" to the outsider with sophisticated agricultural techniques were in fact agricultural lands in the process of regeneration or tribal hunting domains.

Under a regimen of shifting cultivation, effective political power was highly localized until the advent of colonization. The necessities of periodic land preparation meant that political and social cleavages within the group could be resolved through a process of branching out into new areas. This more transient form of settlement made political paramountcy difficult, whether indigenous or external. It is not fortuitous, therefore, that systems of imperial control have generally been coexistive with regions of fixed settlement and peasant agriculture. Rome beyond the Imperial frontiers, Spain in the North American West and the South American Pampas, and Britain on the frontiers of the Indian Empire, all found it more difficult to control nomads and primitive agriculturalists than to dominate more sophisticated settled peoples. In fact, the problem of control generally allowed for only two alternatives: permanent settlement where feasible, or repeated punitive expeditions.

PEASANT AGRICULTURE AND SOCIAL SYSTEMS

Permanent settlement is predicated on a highly productive agricultural base. The technological prerequisites for these levels of productivity vary from region to region. Climate, geography, ecological variables, and cultural traditions present a number of alternatives, a variety of "givens" from which to erect societies based on settled styles of life and continuous agricultural exploitation. Naturally, such factors as precipitation, the potentials of irrigation, and the availability of native or imported animal and plant stocks fit for domestication all make substantial differences in patterns of settled agriculture. Nevertheless, there is a broad commonality in settled agricultural practices of a traditional type sufficient to allow us to recognize it as a conceptual unity, a cultural and technological complex best subsumed under the term, "peasantry."

We would stress, though, that the chief distinction is not between peasant agriculture as a technological form and slash-and-burn agriculture as previously described. Slash-and-burn is a *technique* of cultivation; the peasantry represent a social and cultural type associated with a more encompassing web of social relations—ties to a society of which the peasant aggregate constitutes but one part. While under exceptional circumstances slash-and-burn agriculture can produce sufficient surpluses to achieve population concentrations and large-scale territorial integration, this result can most readily be attained when the slash-and-burn system is anchored to a non-slash-and-burn crop or when shifting cultivators are tied to an external urban-dominated society. One of the most notable examples of a high culture erected on a slash-and-burn foundation is that of the Classic Maya of Middle America. In Africa arboreal crops, such as the plantain and cacao, have acted as anchor points for populations otherwise engaged in slash-and-burn.

The predominant pattern in peasant societies is the stable mixed agricultural farmstead generally grouped in a village complex. Although the focus of social and ritual life, as well as the division of labor, are at the village level, the peasant is forced to deal with economic and political systems and religious forms, all of which are regional or national in scope. The peasant must cope with these external systems, even though he may consider them alien and sometimes malevolent. The policeman, the tax-collector, and the magistrate all are the representatives of the outside world. These agents, by their attitude to those under their jurisdiction—an attitude that is typically one of condescension and superiority—account for much of the distrust and dislike that peasant peoples have toward centralized authority.

These attitudes are reinforced by peasant fears of all that lies beyond the ken of personal relationships. Thus village rivalries, family antagonisms, and land squabbles are commonplace in peasant societies.

To survive, the peasant has had to resort to devious stratagems of noncooperation and institutionalized ignorance. While providing an element of protection under oppressive social and cultural conditions, these same attitudes hamper the efforts of progressive governments and other external agents of modernization. Rarely can the peasant distinguish between the rapacious official and the schoolteacher or public health authority. This lack of differentiation is not without reason; a census taker could be gathering information for military conscription, labor recruitment, or taxation, or conversely, obtaining data vital for the implementation of economic and social development. Similarly, the doctor's interrogation may be understood, not as a basic foundation for therapy, but as information potentially useful for witchcraft.

The official generally has preconceptions of peasant life. For the most part, officials are of a different social class, sometimes even of a different cultural or racial group. The myth of peasant stupidity and childishness is deeply rooted among the elites of traditional societies. Authoritarian behavior is therefore rationalized in terms of the stern (but "benevolent") father enforcing discipline and preserving order. For his part, the peasant plays the role that is expected of him and reinforces this stereotype.

The economic and social position of peasant groups is cogently summarized in A. L. Kroeber's famous observation that:

Peasants are definitely rural—yet live in relation to market towns; they form a class segment of a larger population which usually contains also urban centers, sometimes metropolitan capitals. They constitute part-societies and part-cultures. They lack the isolation, the political autonomy, and the self-sufficiency of tribal populations; but their local units retain much of their identity, integration, and attachment to soils and cults.[3]

With the exception of essentially autonomous primitive societies, the peasantry has comprised the main agricultural and population

[3] A. L. Kroeber, *Anthropology*, New York, 1948, p. 284.

base of all civilizations from ancient times to the advent of the Industrial Revolution. In fact, peasantry has persisted to the present day in industrial countries.

PEASANT SOCIETY AND THE PROBLEM OF AGRICULTURAL CHANGE

While it is true that peasant societies almost everywhere have been undergoing change, the fact remains that in essence change has been slow and, for the most part, recent and peripheral. That peasants today may wear factory-made clothes and vote in national elections does not necessarily entail basic changes in attitudes. Agricultural practices are closely interlocked with household and village technology, and this complex is imbued throughout with deep-rooted attitudes, values, and rituals.

Although it is fair to regard the peasant as "traditional," it cannot be inferred that he does not desire an improvement in his economic condition. The problem is that specific programs of development may not be perceived as necessary means to achieve a higher standard of living. The major factor in peasant resistance to change is the linkage of instrumental behavior to pervasive value systems. Foster notes that:

In programs of directed culture change, ideas of modesty often constitute serious barriers to some kinds of programs. Medical and public health workers, for example, have been seriously handicapped in their efforts to reduce infant and maternal mortality by widely prevalent ideas about female modesty and the proper relationship of a physician to a pregnant woman. In Moslem countries, in Latin America, and in many other areas, it is quite unthinkable that a man other than a woman's husband should have the degree of intimacy with her required by a gynecological examination.[4]

Among East African herdsmen, prestige and social power is accorded to the owner of extensive herds. The primary consideration is not the quality of the stock, but rather the sheer number of animals. In fact, the practice of slaughtering the choicest animal for feasts and rituals has a long-run deleterious effect on the quality of the stock.

[4] George M. Foster, *Traditional Cultures and the Impact of Technological Change*, New York, 1962, pp. 73–74.

Attempts by government officials to introduce selective breeding and range management have met with little success. In much the same manner, the efforts of extension agents to combat overgrazing among Navaho sheep herders met great resistance. The classic example of the ritually protected cow in India requires no elaboration.

In Europe the early identification of maize with animal feed has precluded its later use as a food staple. Among the Spanish-American farmers of New Mexico an experimental program in crop improvement, while initially successful, proved a failure. New strains of hybrid corn tripled the yield but produced *tortillas* of an unacceptable taste, texture, and color. In Mexico yellow maize, a crop of superior nutritional value, has not displaced local strains because, when used in making *tortillas*, it resulted in *tortillas* "identified with careless cooking, and housewives did not wish to be stigmatized as careless or incompetent cooks."[5]

Peasant diets may seem monotonous to the outsider, particularly to one who has grown up in an urban-cosmopolitan society. Eating habits, like all cultural forms rooted in childhood experience, are charged with emotive connotations and strongly resist change. There is more than a grain of truth in the dictum that nothing is so palatable as mother's cooking. The need for sustenance is a biological imperative, but culture defines what constitutes a proper meal and the form in which it is to be consumed. Mediterranean peasants would no more consider the possibility of a repast without a loaf of bread than Mexican *campesinos* would envisage a meal without the ubiquitous *tortilla*. Describing the diet of the Bemba of then Northern Rhodesia, Audrey Richards observes that:

. . . a man praising porridge made of millet flour often says, "if you have eaten your fill with *ubwali* you do not get hungry quickly again as with other foods." He seems to appreciate the feelings in his stomach and elsewhere which the eating of porridge gives. Anyone who habitually bolts the coarse heavy millet *ubwali* at a rate which the Bemba do probably becomes accustomed to a particular sensation of tension inside. To the European this would amount almost to a pain, but it is evident that the Bemba want to feel full in just this particular way, and do not feel satisfied unless they have reached this state.[6]

[5] Foster, *op. cit.*, pp. 71, 75–76, and Anacleto Apodaco, "Corn and Custom: The Introduction of Hybrid Corn to Spanish American Farmers in New Mexico," in E. H. Spicer, ed., *Human Problems in Technological Change*, New York, 1952, pp. 35–39.

[6] Audrey I. Richards, *Land, Labour and Diet in Northern Rhodesia*, Oxford, 1961, p. 52.

Quite apart from emotional resistances, there are empirical reasons for not accepting certain programs of technical change. For those living on the very margins of subsistence—a condition characteristic of most peasantry—the risks entailed in a new technique of agriculture may be more than they are willing to accept. No matter how imperfect it may appear to the expert, peasant systems of agriculture constitute a time-tested solution to the problems of subsistence. Furthermore, peasant systems of belief rationalize periodic adversities as the natural lot of man. Fatalism is hardly an attitude conducive to experimentation and change. An externally-induced failure is not so easily rationalized and, while it can literally mean life or death to the cultivator, the administrator is likely to suffer little from the loss.

THE ECOLOGY OF AGRICULTURAL CHANGE

The enthusiasm of the visiting expert frequently blinds him to realities that are frequently recognized by the peasant. Intercropping is a common peasant practice. It provides a hedge against famine— one crop may fail—and adds important nutriments and variety to the diet. A single crop (possibily a new strain) will under most circumstances yield more abundantly. But it unbalances the diet and lacks the protection of a multiplicity of cultigens. Furthermore, if single cropping calls for a new variety, it can mean the purchase of seeds, for which the peasant may have to depend on middlemen or moneylenders. Given the prevailing high interest rates in most peasant areas, any increase in agricultural productivity may thus not benefit the peasant.

The agricultural cycle limits the temporal horizon of the peasant. Crops are planted, food is consumed, and a seed-portion retained for the following season. Even if the crop is abundant, limitations of land and labor preclude more extensive cultivation by use of potentially surplus seed. Furthermore, primitive storage systems do not allow bumper years to balance the bad. At least initially, the shift to a single crop and a greater reliance on the market do not uproot this pattern of life. If the ultimate consumer is distant, the vicissitudes of the market compound the uncertainties of nature and confound the peasant with forces he little understands.

The transition to a market economy with a concomitant use of monetary accumulation against bad years is of long standing in many peasant societies. It has been noted as a characteristic of European peasantry. The myth of the frugal European peasant is not without foundation. In other regions, such as India, gold and jewelry serve the same purpose and, incidentally, these small accumulations withhold a valuable source of foreign exchange from the government. It is equally true that in other areas ceremonial and other expenditures use up any accumulated surplus. In all likelihood this tradition of rapid and almost total consumption of surpluses is related to such factors as a temporal horizon limited by the agricultural cycle, lack of social mobility, and the possibility of periodic breakdown in law and order. When these cultural attitudes persist into a present in which they are dysfunctional, a reorientation must precede economic progress.

There are concrete technological reasons, other than those directly related to cultivation, that make change difficult to accept. Agricultural specialists rarely study the household technology, yet methods of preparation are inseparable from techniques of food production. Regardless of cultural taste biases, the absence of technologies related to particular foodstuffs may preclude their use. During the Irish potato famine, even "when meal and flour reached their destination, difficulties remained. Many of the inhabitants had never tasted bread; their kitchens had no ovens; the housewives did not know how to make loaves."[7] While in due course this barrier was overcome, the interim price in human suffering was great. Manioc, now a widely diffused tropical staple, spread slowly as a result of the complex nature of the technology used in expressing its lethal prussic acid.[8]

The food resources that form the diet of peasant and simple societies frequently have a variety of other uses inherent in the maintenance of the economy. In Northern Nigeria, Guinea corn (sorghum) normally reaches a height of 10–12 feet.

The dry stems are used for fuel, basket and mat making and a variety of structural purposes, and as stakes for climbing plants such as yams, gourds and beans. Green leaves can be used as fodder for livestock. The entire crop can be cut for direct feeding, silage or hay.[9]

If the supremacy of traditional crops is to be challenged, obviously it is imperative that substitutes be found for the myriad products

[7] Marcus Lee Hansen, *The Atlantic Migration 1607–1860*, New York, 1961, p. 248.

[8] William O. Jones, *Manioc in Africa*, Stanford, 1959.

[9] International Bank for Reconstruction and Development, *Economic Development of Nigeria*, Baltimore, 1956, p. 246.

based on these crops. To some degree, substitution has already occurred in the form of machine-made products; it is the exceptional contemporary peasant household that does not command a modicum of factory-made goods. But it is equally exceptional to encounter peasants who do not, to some degree, rely on local or domestic handicrafts.

Peasant ingenuity is also apparent in the novel use of the debris of Western technology. A visitor to rural Mexico can observe the extent to which old tires constitute the raw material for the typical country sandal, the *huarache*. Throughout much of the underdeveloped world the skills of the local tinker have been applied to fashioning cooking utensils, lamps, tools, and so on, from discarded metal containers. The junkheap of industrial society is a veritable mine for the peasant. Paradoxically, many a tourist brings home these products as typical examples of native handicrafts.

In some cases the impact of factory-made goods plus the use of substitute materials and techniques by peasant artisans have led to the decline or disappearance of native craft tradition.

Despite these marginal adaptations of Western technology by peasant peoples, the core of modern technology cannot be adopted by peasant groups without expert assistance. Basically, complex technology is founded on a body of knowledge and experience alien to their way of life.

If due account is taken of the cultural and environmental factors we have discussed, then scientific and technological research may make a great contribution to the progressive development of peasant agriculture. With few exceptions, peasant diets lack some vital nutritional elements. Particularly serious is the position of young children—from weaning to about five or six years of age—who have difficulty digesting some of the foodstuffs that provide an element of balance to the adult diet. Infants in most peasant societies are not weaned until they are two years or older and consequently enjoy a more balanced diet than their older siblings. These older children must subsist on an essentially adult diet for which their digestive systems are unprepared. At this critical age they are also subjected to diseases carried in food and utensils for which they have as yet been unable to develop a high level of resistance.

Oscar Lewis has observed that for the Mexican village of Tepotzlan:

Illness and death are frequent in children after weaning. Often the illness or death is attributed to indigestion or *ético* (consumption) in which the child wastes away. These are associated with the changed diet of the child at weaning, and it is highly probable that these children do not

receive sufficient nourishment, or are given foods unsuited to the digestive systems of young children. Many women wean *con pura tortilla*, that
is with inadequate food substitutes. These children are shifted to the diet
of the adult, which consists of *tortilla*, beans or bean soup, rice or noodles
prepared with much lard or oil, and black coffee. In some families children
of two are also permitted to eat *chile* and various local seeds which whether
toasted or raw, are difficult to digest.[10]

It is fair to point out that some elements of children's diets, while
running counter to the dietary preconceptions of outside observers
and officials, may in fact be functional in the cultural context of the
peoples in question. As water is generally contaminated, the drinking
of black coffee by children (Mexican, Navaho, and so on) provides an
element of protection that plain water lacks. Similarly, while we may
view alcoholic beverages primarily as intoxicants, wine, beer, and
similar beverages are staple foods of high nutritional value consumed
by both children and adults in many peasant cultures. Quite apart
from palatability, alcoholic beverages have a keeping quality that
their raw material constituents lack.

EDUCATION AND THE POTENTIAL OF
MODERN SCIENCE AND TECHNOLOGY

Under the influence of education and the spread of public health
and better dietary knowledge, the diets of some of the better situated
peasants are improving. Specific research is being conducted to make
available nutritious and balanced foods falling within the economic
range of low income peoples. One of the most promising research
developments has been aimed at the fuller exploitation of the world's
fish resources. Fish meal, tasteless, high in proteins, capable of being
stored and transported without refrigeration, has already been successfully manufactured in pilot plants and is available for full-scale
production. Among the virtues of this product is the total utilization
of the fish and of species of fish that would not otherwise be commercially marketable. The fact that fish meal is tasteless gives it the
potential of being added to traditional foods—breads, soups, por-
ridges—without disrupting cultural food habits.

[10] Oscar Lewis, *Life in a Mexican Village: Tepotzlan Revisited*, Urbana,
Ill., 1963, p. 377.

Substantial progress has already been made in making available powdered milk for school children and nursing mothers in under-developed countries. In many areas, such as West Africa, indigenous vegetable oils are being used to reconstitute powdered milk, thus making it more nutritious.

Many programs of rural development require the active partner-ship of the peasant. New varieties of seeds have been developed that not only produce a more abundant yield but also have greater resistance to blights. In years past, cocoa and cotton have been par-ticularly vulnerable to disease. The introduction of more resistant strains has allowed a greater continuity of production and assured the peasant of at least some market income. Improved seeds and their treatment by chemical agents have also greatly benefitted the peasant who produces primarily for himself and the local market. In Tanzania increased yields of 50 percent for sesame, 25 percent for cotton, and 10 percent for soya beans have followed the introduction of new seeds. In a nation whose yearly per capita income is between $40–50, increments of this range provide not only a vital addition to foreign exchange but also that climate of success conducive to further in-novation and experimentation.

In many cases the yield from hybrid corn is double that achieved from other strains. Since corn forms the staple of so many peasant diets, the successful introduction of hybrid corn can be expected to have great benefits. Other opportunities for comparable increment exist in rice, another staple of the underdeveloped world. The effort and care expended in the cultivation of rice is sufficiently known so as not to require elaborate documentation, yet the productivity of wet rice agriculture in Asia compares unfavorably not only to European wet rice cultivation (Po Valley, Ebro Delta, and so on) but also to North America's, with its more extensive agricultural practices. For example, in 1963–1964 the yields were (in units of 1000 metric tons per 1000 hectares): 5.24 for Japan, 5.12 for Italy, 4.43 for the United States, 2.28 for Malaysia, 1.59 for Thailand, 1.55 for Burma, 1.54 for India, and 1.20 for Cambodia.[11] Needless to say, these greater yields for Western agriculture can be attributed not only to improved seeds but also to other advanced agricultural practices, although it must be admitted that some of the low yielding rice strains are more nutritious.

[11] *F.A.O. Monthly Bulletin of Agricultural Economies and Statistics*, De-cember 1964, Vol. 13, p. 30. Figures are an approximation only.

Fish resources and their potential for expansion

Other more radical innovations will require long-term cooperation between the peasant and outside technical experts. Great possibilities exist for the development of inland fishery resources. There are many lowland areas that could be blocked off and permanently inundated for fish farming. A native of the African lakes, the talapia fish has proved adaptable to a variety of tropical environments. It has great nutritional value and multiplies rapidly. Talapia and other species can be introduced into existing streams, lakes, and paddy fields, thus enriching food resources without changing the systems of environmental exploitation. It is obvious that scientifically managed fish farms demand a much higher degree of interaction and continuous cooperation between inhabitants and professional experts.

With few exceptions most fishermen can be considered as belonging to the peasantry. Even in highly industrialized countries the individuals employed in highly sophisticated fishing fleets frequently conserve peasant values and attitudes. Depending upon the circumstances, fishermen find themselves in conditions comparable to that of peasants cultivating cash crops or working on a plantation.[12]

The coastal Japanese have long exploited a broad range of marine resources. In addition to fish and sea mammals they gather a variety of seaweed and algae. Seaweed is used as an ingredient in soups and vegetable dishes and as a seasoning. Kelps contain monosodium glutamate, a recent addition to Western prestige cooking. Algae find their place in Japanese cuisine as condiments, garnishes, jellies, soup stocks, preservatives, and vinegared dishes. These products constitute about 5 percent of total Japanese marine consumption. According to the Japanese microbiologist, Atsushi Watanabe:

This amount may appear rather insignificant, but some of the algae are rather rich in protein and contain important amounts of vitamins and minerals. For instance, the algae sheet of *Porphyra tenera* is rich in B vitamins, provitamin A, and vitamin C. Among the various minerals contained in the seaweeds (iron, copper, calcium, manganese, iodine, etc.), the abundance of iodine deserves special mention because it is considered to be the main reason for the rarity of goiter among the Japanese people.[13]

[12] It is interesting to note the persistence of peasant themes among the fishermen of Greek, Portuguese, and Italian extraction along the Eastern seaboard of the United States.

[13] Atsushi Watanabe, "Algae as Foodstuff," in Ruth Gruber, ed., *Science in the New Nations*, New York, 1961, p. 146.

Apart from their nutritional qualities, some algae are nitrogen-fixing and consequently have the same beneficial effect upon the soil as leguminous plants. They may be directly used as fertilizer, and experiments are being conducted in Japan on their feasibility as cattle and poultry fodder. In India and other parts of Southeast Asia, natural strains of nitrogen-fixing algae have been discovered in paddy fields. The presence of these organisms accounts, at least partially, for the sustained fertility of those rice fields in which they are found.

Fish farming and the use of seaweed and algae have only had a local or regional impact. As fertilizers, the main barrier to the introduction of algae and seaweed is the technical problem of providing them to the peasant at a low cost or of devising a method for the peasant to propagate algae continuously. As food, fish, seaweed, and algae will encounter the type of cultural resistance that we have already noted. The fish resources off the coasts of India are substantial; nevertheless, traditional dietary beliefs have precluded their effective utilization among a people who are seriously deficient in protein. These conditions are essentially duplicated in Latin America, the difference being that disdain for fish is not postulated on religious belief. On the contrary, the traditions of the Catholic Church favor the eating of fish on Friday. So strong was this disdain that certain parts of Latin America—including some maritime regions—were exempted from the prohibition of eating meat on Friday.

LOCAL ORGANIZATION AND THE DIFFUSION OF TECHNOLOGY

The diffusion of complex techniques and methods demands more than individual conversions; it requires the presence of a functioning autochthonous organization willing and able to receive assistance and disseminate it to its members. While the structure of peasant communities is not uniform from area to area—varying from rigid hierarchy to communal democracy—the practice of joint decision making and collective action is to some degree a peasant universal. The maintenance of the peasant community as a viable entity demands concerted effort. In the face of the outside world, internal cleavages are subordinated to the overriding objectives of community preservation.

These local organizations present both a problem and a promise for social change. In origin they can be understood in part as bound-ary-maintaining mechanisms. The more rigidly hierarchical structures are a particular problem, since those in seats of power have a vested interest in the status quo. Even in the more internally flexible systems, change may be strongly resisted because of previous harsh experience with external authority or present emotional fears.

However, the fact that peasant communities in large part function on a cooperative basis offers a foundation for the erection of local organizations geared to modernization. This potential has often been vitiated by outsiders who have attempted to impose their concepts of what a cooperative should be. A local cooperative requires social control over those in positions of responsibility as well as clear channels of communication. That many cooperatives, both in format and in their allocation of positions of power, obviously represent the constructs of the bureaucratic mind results in a failure to act as genuine cooperative enterprises. Thus, the Mexican *ejidal* system is formally based on *comunidades agrarias* but has in most instances evolved into *de facto* individual land holdings. Even when cooperatives have had a modicum of success in diffusing modern technology, they have frequently failed because of graft and corruption. Individual office holders did not feel bound by the constraints of traditional peasant society; similarly, the rank and file considered the organization (viewed as foreign and impersonal) fair game for dishonesty and chicanery.

Nevertheless, cooperatives or community development programs can be an important vehicle for disseminating modern technology and engendering social and economic change. It must be realized, however, that peasant systems cannot be immediately overhauled and that in all programs of change great consideration must be given to local and specific conditions. While peasant life has much in common the world over, there is a broad spectrum of variation. Objective scientific and technical knowledge is certainly the foundation of Western industrialization and high standards of living. Too often, though, the Western expert takes for granted the cultural and environmental context of his discipline and assumes that organizational forms and specific techniques are universally valid. This difficulty is compounded by the brief tenure of visiting experts.

There is no substitute for continuous close observation; then, and only then, comes the application of the specialist's knowledge to the solution of local problems. After all, this approach is in the best tradition of science: observation, experimentation, observation of results, and correction. Among the most noted examples of successful community action are the Kilimanjaro Native Cooperative Union and the Cornell Peru Project at Hacienda Vicos. The K.N.C.U. had the benefit of an English agricultural officer willing to nurture a small marketing group into a full-fledged cooperative that not only grows and markets coffee but also has built roads and erected schools and hospitals. A. L. B. Bennet, who first arrived in Tanganyika in 1921, was seconded as administrative officer of the association in 1930 and was still among the Chaga when Tanganyika gained its independence in 1961. This is not to imply that a single expert must spend decades in the field in order to generate successful development, but it indicates that major restructuring of peasant economic systems cannot be achieved by junketeering experts.

The Vicos experiment further underlines the fact that time, patience, and understanding are the essential ingredients of successful outside assistance. The origins of the Cornell Peru Project date shortly after the Second World War, when the Vicos area was selected by anthropologist Allan R. Holmberg as a locality for the study of Andean peasantry. After five years of preparatory investigation under the auspices of the University of San Marcos and the Smithsonian Institution, the Vicos project was launched in cooperation with the Peruvian Indian Institute. For generations, the hacienda of Vicos had been owned by the government, which periodically leased it to the highest bidder. The Indians were in a basically feudal relationship to the *patrón* of the manor. Being dependent on the holder of a lease, Vicosiños found it possible to relate to the last of a series of *patrones*, Cornell, in terms of traditional patterns of behavior. For their part, the Cornell experts had no choice but to enter the structure of society other than in a role understood by local inhabitants. The fact that in 1956, five years after the formal initiation of the program, Cornell was able to abandon its position of *patrón*, testifies to the fact that this was a progressive policy. Since then, Cornell has remained in an advisory capacity to a locally self-governing community with control over land and resources.

The traditional crops of the Andean highlands, corn and potatoes, have remained the staples of the Vicos agricultural economy. Initially, blight-resistant potato seeds and improved techniques of cultivation were made available to those families willing to accept them. Potato production rapidly increased, and more families joined the project. While important, especially in terms of its demonstration effect, the introduction of improved strains could be accomplished within the context of the existing social conditions. Once the potato crop was established, each year's seeds could be supplied from a portion of the previous harvest.

With traditional distrust of outsiders reduced and with success as a stimulus for innovation, the Vicosiños were primed for the more difficult step of planting hybrid corn and making the structural adjustments involved in shifting to a more commercial agriculture. The Vicos system as it has developed combines family farming together with cooperative enterprise on some 15 percent of the land under cultivation. Though a small part of the total holdings, the communal cultivation has been an important source of experimentation and the diffusion of new techniques. The practical gains of an improved system of agriculture have manifested themselves in a higher individual standard of living but also in a vastly expanded program of education and public health.[14]

In both Kilimanjaro and Vicos we have a situation that obviously cannot be considered the normative pattern for community development throughout the world. At Kilimanjaro a dedicated civil servant, supported by a trained Chaga senior clerk, willingly devoted three decades of effort to the task of cooperative development. With respect to Vicos, a team of American experts, aided by Peruvian colleagues and a university-trained Vicosiño, worked at the dual tasks of stimulating change in a community and forging tools for directed economic and social development. From its inception, Vicos was intended as a laboratory for applied anthropology.

From these and other similar projects some operational principles have been established which, if used judiciously, can provide a base line for programs of economic development. Such projects should not require the massive support or long-term assistance that have characterized Vicos and Kilimanjaro. Given the scarcity of skilled manpower and the enormity of the development task, it is patently impossible to have a Vicos-type experiment in every peasant village.

The Vicos experiment has already facilitated the transformation of other villages in the Peruvian Altiplano. The tangible results of the Vicos experiment have already demonstrated to surrounding communities the benefits that can be derived from planned social change. One of the incidental benefits of a higher standard of living among the Vicosiños has been increased geographical mobility, which has helped to disseminate the idea that economic improvement is possible. The principles learned from Vicos can most readily be applied to Andean communities with shared cultural characteristics. In other areas, caution must be exercised in adapting the Vicos principles to differing cultural and ecological contexts.

[14] Henry F. Dobyns, *The Social Matrix of Peruvian Indigenous Communities*, Ithaca, N.Y., 1964, p. 78.

BIBLIOGRAPHY

Biebuyck, Daniel (ed.), *African Agrarian Systems*, London, 1963.

Burling, Robbins, *Hill Farms and Padi Fields*, Englewood Cliffs, N.J., 1965.

de Schlippe, Pierre, *Shifting Cultivation in Africa*, London, 1956.

de Wilde, John C., et al., *Agricultural Development of Tropical Africa*, Volumes 1 and 2, Baltimore, 1967.

Dumont, René, *False Start in Africa*, New York, 1966.

Evans-Pritchard, E. E., *The Nuer*, London, 1940.

Gourou, Pierre, *The Tropical World*, London, 1961.

Gray, Robert F., *The Sonja of Tanganyika*, London, 1963.

Kimble, George H. T., *Tropical Africa: Vol. I. Land and Livelihood*, New York, 1960.

La Anyane, S., *Ghana Agriculture*, London, 1963.

Nash, Manning, *Primitive and Peasant Economic Systems*, San Francisco, 1966.

Scudder, Thayer, *The Ecology of the Gwembe Tonga*, Manchester, 1962.

Smith T. Lynn (ed.), *Agrarian Reform in Latin America*, New York, 1965.

Wolf, Eric R., *Peasants*, Englewood Cliffs, N.J., 1966.

Yudelman, Montague, *Africans on the Land*, Cambridge, Mass., 1964

IV

Peasant Village and National Culture

THE STRUCTURE OF THE VILLAGE

The village is the arena of peasant social life. Typically, village inhabitants are known to one another on the basis of shared experience in work, ritual, and recreation. A system structured on face-to-face relationships is difficult to maintain when population size exceeds the limits beyond which the individual can know with ease the relevant information concerning the other members of the community. Beyond some 1500 inhabitants the village loses some of its cohesion, and tendencies toward social segmentation can be expected to emerge. Villagers may have personal ties with individuals outside the community, but whether the links are in-village or out-village, an upper ceiling is imposed on the number of such relationships. The goal is to tap all possible sources of aid and cooperation and in so doing to assure a degree of security in an existence largely devoid of power and influence. As George M. Foster writes of Tzintzuntzan (Mexico) in particular, and peasant environments in general:

Ego looks for ways to interest and obligate potential partners, both colleagues and patrons, whom he feels can help him, and in so doing, commits himself to carry out the terms of the bargain with those who, in effect, accept his offer. By means of a great number of dyadic contacts, with both

64

colleagues and patrons, the villager maximizes his security in the uncertain world in which he lives.[1]

As previously indicated, the national power structure is external to the village, and resident agents of control and authority tend to be recruited from outside the community. Police officers (except for local constables with limited powers), magistrates, revenue agents, and in some cases the clergy may live in the village, but are seldom perceived as members of the community either by themselves or the inhabitants. Rural aristocracies, when present, do share with villagers long established ties to the locality, but again, differences in class (or caste) membership and cultural orientation preclude a really close identity of interest with the peasantry. Village society proper, therefore, can best be viewed as a truncated social structure encompassing only the subordinate elements of the national social and political system.

Nevertheless, there is a considerable variety in peasant societies. In some cases—southern Europe and Latin American are good examples—village endogamy is pretty well the norm; on the other hand, south Asian villages typically are broken up into a number of occupational and caste groupings that require for their perpetuation a substantial degree of intervillage (but intragroup) marriage.

Substantial differences can also be observed in economic organization. The Indian villages of Mexico and Guatemala are nearly all centers of a given craft tradition: pottery making, textiles, the production of wooden utensils, copper working, etc. These articles constitute the stock-in-trade for a system of interchange geared to specific market days in a circuit of villages.[2] Much the same situation is encountered in Bali, where "in one hamlet almost everyone manufactures musical instruments, or works silver or manufactures salt, or weaves, or makes pots, or produces coconut oil."[3] In other culture areas, village communities appear to be economically more self-sufficient and a whole range of specialists may be domiciled within the village. Hindu India is generally a good example of such a pattern. A broad range of specialists may contribute to a situation, such as

[1] George M. Foster, "The Dyadic Contract in Tzintzuntzan, II: Patron Client Relationship," *American Anthropologist*, Vol. 65, No. 6, 1966, p. 1293.

[2] Lilly de Jongh Osborne, *Indian Crafts of Guatemala and El Salvador*, Norman, Oklahoma, 1965; Bronislaw Malinowski and Julio de la Fuente, "La economía de un sistema de mercados en México," *Acta Anthropologica*, Época 2, Vol. 1, No. 2, México, D.F., 1957.

[3] Clifford Geertz, *Peddlars and Princes: Social Development and Economic Change in Two Indonesian Towns*, Chicago, 1963, p. 89.

the one Rani Khera in the Delhi district, in which something under fifty percent of the families engage in primary activities (craft and ceremonial) that are other than agricultural.[4]

Naturally, differences in the modalities of marriage and social organization—including the economic sphere—affect the structure of village life and the forms and degree of interaction between villagers and outsiders. Thus, village communities may be more or less isolated from national or religious "great traditions." In Hindu villages, "the festivals of Sanskritic rationale and nomenclature provide, along with domestic ceremonies, the principal occasions on which most villagers may engage in concerted symbolic activities."[5] While the festivals of the Christian calendar give some common frame of reference to village life in Latin America and Southern Europe, it is notable that major festivals (other than those geared to rites of passage) tend to be dedicated to local patron saints and are therefore observances whose importance is mainly restricted to a given locality.

There is consequently a considerable range of variation in degrees of village isolation as measured by such factors as economic interdependence, patterns of kinship and marriage, and the extent to which higher order traditions penetrate the peasant community. Obviously, a high level of village craft specialization must go together with a well-defined system of interchange, but it does not follow that contacts and relationships of one type facilitate other forms of interaction. In fact, market-oriented Mesoamerican Indian communities are also characterized by a high degree of village endogamy; one may trade but not marry. Also, it should not be assumed that high levels of interaction indicate close links with the national culture. Again, to cite the Mesoamerican case, it should be noted that with the partial exception of agricultural produce, the goods produced by villages move along a transactional web that barely touches the national economy. In a few exceptional instances, such as the town of Tonalá near Guadalajara in Mexico, the growing interest of upper class urbanites and foreign tourists in folk handicrafts has led to a situation in which old patterns of production persist, but the goods are mainly channeled into national and international markets.[6]

[4] Oscar Lewis, "Peasant Culture in India and Mexico: A Comparative Analysis," *Village India: Studies in the Little Community*, McKim Marriott, ed., Memoir 83 of the American Anthropological Association, 1955, p. 151.

[5] McKim Marriott, "Little Communities in An Indigenous Civilization," *Village India: Studies in the Little Community, op. cit.*, p. 193.

[6] May N. Diaz, *Tonalá: Conservatism, Responsibility, and Authority in a Mexican Town*, Berkeley and Los Angeles, 1966, pp. 168–189. The craftsmen of Tonalá sell a high percentage of their pottery to the State Ceramic

PEASANT COMMUNITIES, CLASS, STRUCTURES, AND NATIONAL LIFE

At a more general level, peasant communities as components of larger national aggregates are necessarily linked to their respective national cultures through organizational forms that are in part national and in part local. Class-based social structures predominate in Southern Europe, Latin America, and in some regions of Asia. Seen from the outside—that is, in contrast to the directing sectors of the national culture—village communities may give the appearance of a sort of equality in poverty, the external observer finding it difficult to distinguish between individual levels of wealth among the peasantry. Yet, in most instances, villagers recognize relative levels of affluence—the extra cow, the fraction of a hectare, perhaps even the ownership of a few almond trees.

There is no denying that for peasants on the verge of subsistence, small increments of wealth are matters of major importance. It would hardly be valid, however, to view peasant communities as internally stratified by class.[7] Peasants tend to recognize their class membership and, in turn, the middle and upper classes make fairly rigid distinctions. Wealth is but one criterion of class membership. It is possible to find individual peasants, peasant families, or even substantial segments of peasant communities, who on the basis of pure wealth are more affluent than sectors of the national middle class. In terms of way of life, education, and general cultural orientation, there nevertheless remain discontinuities that preclude classifying such individuals and groups as fully integrated components of the national culture. This point is clearly brought out in Laurence Wylie's *A Village in Vaucluse*, a study of a prosperous community of peasant smallholders in southeastern France. It is evident that these peasants look with suspicion on the outside world, especially the official world of government, statute law, and formal education. "The identity of the outside *ils* (they) varies . . . Usually, however, it refers to the

---

Museum of Tlaquepaque and indirectly to the Museo de Artes Populares in Mexico City. Private entrepreneurship may also lead to a broadening of traditional markets; see, for instance, Michael Belshaw, *A Village Economy: Land and People of Huecorio*, New York, 1967, pp. 221–227.

[7] Reference is to the peasantry proper, not to the agents of national or metropolitan culture or resident landed gentry.

French Government in all its manifestations, for it is the government which collects taxes, makes war, controls the wine production, and employs impersonal civil servants."[8] Peyrane, the community in question, is hardly to be taken as typical of peasant society, for it enjoys a level of prosperity that ranks high for France as a whole. Yet in terms of identity, class, and culture, these are true peasants.

In a static economy the peasant segments of class systems can appear quite rigid. Class lines, once established, tend to be self-perpetuating. Values and attitudes are formed, and expectations and activities are defined by class position. Membership in the peasant class inhibits mobility and serves as a protective device to preserve group integrity, personal and family resources and, to some degree, the capacity for joint action. To the peasant, communal solidarity, if only in the form of passive nonacceptance, offers a shield against exploitation and the vagaries of an ill-understood external world. Easy exit is a threat to the group, and therefore the barriers of class should be understood as being maintained both from within and without. Thus, the individual peasant who attempts to break out of his class of origin faces the suspicions of his group as well as the hostility of the class to which he aspires. The boundary-maintaining mechanisms of peasant society need not necessarily reflect contemporary conditions and dangers; it is sufficient that past experience be such as to have instilled suspicion of the outside world and any involvement with it.

Nevertheless, class systems, even preindustrial ones, do exhibit an element of flexibility. Class is in part geared to economic factors, and the categories involved are consequently less ascriptive than in organizational forms based on caste or lineage. It is true that in a class society the new rich may remain tainted by lowly origins, but if wealth is retained and sufficient motivation is present, time provides the universal solvent. It is also not uncommon to find successful urbanites retaining residual ties with localities of origin. The periodic return to the village is a ritual performed by many urban dwellers in societies undergoing urbanization and technological change.[9] Emotional ties of this type do not preclude an everyday

[8] Laurence Wylie, *Village in the Vaucluse: An Account of Life in a French Village*, New York, 1964, p. 206. See also Chapters 7 and 10.

[9] The periodic, often yearly, return to the village of origin is especially pronounced in southern Europe. A tendency for new urbanites to retain links with their extended families and localities of birth has also been noted for Japan. See Edwin Johnson, "The Stem Family and Its Extension in Present Day Japan," *American Anthropologist*, Vol. 66, No. 4, Part 1, 1964, pp. 844–848.

contempt for the peasant, alloyed, perhaps, with myths of the virtues and simplicities of rural life. To a substantial degree this may be understood as a form of rationalization: peasants are happy in their lot, they are free of the stresses and strains of urban life, and their codes of behavior, while simple and innocent, represent something old and original in the human condition, virtues that have been lost by the affluent and educated city dweller and the landed aristocracy.

CASTE SYSTEMS

Caste as a system of stratification is manifested in its most extreme forms in Hindu India. The chief characteristic of such a system is the presence of a "hierarchy of endogamous divisions in which membership is hereditary and permanent."[10] Exactly how permanent and hereditary caste membership turns out to be depends on how in fact (as distinct from cultural fiction) the barriers of caste are insurmountable and at what point the barriers are drawn, for even in caste systems there exist differences in the thresholds that separate particular castes and subcastes. What must be recognized is that, compared to class systems, caste organizations are much more directly linked to the accidents of birth and ascriptive membership.

As a phenomenon, the concept of caste should not be limited to the forms prevalent in southern Asia. Caste situations are recognizable in Latin America, parts of Africa, Japan, the West Indies, and portions of the United States, as well as in India and areas contiguous to it. As a system of stratification, caste may, and very often does, operate conjointly with principles of class alignment. The vestiges of fedualism in Southern Europe, even today, give rise to situations that must be understood in terms of caste as well as class. Describing the social stratification of a southern Italian village, Leonard Moss and Stephen C. Cappannari observe that:

Upward mobility is possible but difficult. If the son of a peasant were to become a physician (unlikely but within the realm of possibility) he would not be admitted to membership in the upper class. He still remains the son of a contadino (peasant). While he is considered as above his class of origin, he is not a member of the class to which he aspires.

[10] Gerald D. Berreman, "Caste in India and the United States," *American Journal of Sociology*, Vol. 66, No. 1960, p. 120.

Class endogamy is rigidly fixed in the values of the community. Only once in recent years has there been an attempt to marry out of one's class. The daughter of one of the signorotti married the son of a merchant. The daughter was disinherited by her father and his home was closed to her and her offspring.[11]

When the barriers of class are so rigid, and the norms of endogamy so strictly kept, it is questionable whether the situation can best be described as one of caste or class.[12]

Theoretically, the barriers of caste in India are insurmountable; in practice it has proved possible for individuals to operate in areas of activity where caste lines take on less importance. State bureaucracies, the military, the educational system, and large scale industry; all offer avenues for individual and family advancement. In these areas of national life, a class system is steadily eroding and displacing traditional alignments.

Time, too, has altered the relationships and the hierarchical ordering of Hindu castes, although caste and subcaste endogamy has proved more resistant. Improvements in the fortunes of particular subcastes has generally led to claims of higher status and at times made for considerable intergroup friction.

Outside of India, caste structures are for the most part associated with colonial situations or the aftermath of colonial experiences. Even in India, caste appears to have its distant origins in conquest, and certainly the system lent itself to the superimposition of new conquest structures, first by Muslim invaders and later by the British. The latter governed the Indian Empire as a ruling caste of guardians separated from the populace by differences of ethnic origin, language, and culture.

In Latin America the Spaniards (and also the Portuguese) established a system of socio-racial stratification from which the English term (via Portuguese Goa) is actually derived. In Spanish and Portuguese, *casta* initially referred to what might be called "breeding," and *castizo* implied pride in social and religious origins of an approved nature. Not unlike the Hindu situation, a tendency toward fragmentation into subcastes is discernible, one authority listing a total of forty-six different *castas* in late colonial Mexico, although it

[11] Leonard Moss and Stephen C. Cappannari, "Estate and Class in a South Italian Hill Village," *American Anthropologist*, Vol. 64, No. 2, 1962, p. 293.

[12] For a somewhat different example of a caste-like situation in Eastern Europe, see Mark Zborowski and Elizabeth Herzog, *Life is With People: The Culture of the Shtetl*, New York, 1962, pp. 421–430.

is unlikely that such minute distinctions were ever socially signifi-cant.[13] In the southern United States and the West Indies a caste and class system evolved with group membership closely related to the racial and social separation of masters and slaves.[14] In Africa, European conquest and colonization erected a caste system that persists in the Republic of South Africa and Rhodesia.

In localities where caste has become an integral part of society, such as India, Latin America, and to a certain degree the southern United States, it often acts as an effective barrier to technological change. However, throughout most of Africa, where the caste struc-ture is of relatively recent imposition, its rapid dismantling in the wake of decolonization may result in the repatriation or expulsion of individuals with technological skills not otherwise available in the society. Certainly caste-like systems hinder the spread of knowledge, but regardless of this long-run effect, the fact remains that the resolution of economic and technological problems in contemporary Africa and some other excolonial areas will require the presence of expatriate personnel for some years to come. Needless to say, this should not be taken as a brief for the perpetuation of caste arrange-ments but rather as a plea for careful dismantling and steady trans-formation of the economic systems inherited by newly emergent na-tions.

As noted, India can count on a national component in her social structure that exhibits a degree of flexibility and independence from the dictates of caste. Unfortunately, this component penetrates but marginally at the village level where human action remains largely caste oriented. Students of Indian society are also aware that caste has not only reinforced urban-rural cleavages, but, given the fact that caste is still far from absent in the middle and upper reaches of urban society, it has contributed to a certain lack of integration, a certain lack of common purpose, in national life.[15] It remains true

[13] Joaquin Roncal, "The Negro Race in Mexico," *The Hispanic American Historical Review*, Vol. 24, No. 3, 1944, p. 533; Oriol Pi-Sunyer, "Historical Background to the Negro in Mexico," *The Journal of Negro History*, Vol. XLII, No. 4, 1957, p. 11ff.; George Kubler, *The Indian Caste of Peru, 1795–1940: A Population Study Based Upon Tax Records and Census Reports*, Washington, 1952.

[14] Oscar and Mary F. Handlin, "Origins of the Southern Labor System," *William and Mary Quarterly*, April 1950; Barton M. Schwartz, "Caste and Endogamy in Trinidad," *Southwestern Journal of Anthropology*, Vol. 20, No. 1, 1964; Leo A. Despres, "The Implications of Nationalist Politics in British Guiana for the Development of Cultural Theory," *American Anthropologist*, Vol. 66, No. 5, 1964, pp. 1062–1063.

[15] Dhirendra Narain, "Indian National Character in the Twentieth Cen-

that, to the extent that Indian society offers avenues of mobility and opportunities for change, these are to be encountered primarily outside the setting of the village community.

Village settlement patterns in India reflect caste divisions, castes and subcastes being grouped geographically in specific quarters or neighborhoods. Although the traditional rural political structure does have features of representative, or at least collegiate, government, such as the election of village elders for posts on the *panchayat* (council), effective leadership, or sometimes simply effective control, tends to be monopolized by prestigious individuals of superordinate castes. The major source of wealth, land, is often in the hands of dominant castes, while other castes or subcastes may be denied land or even the opportunity of working it.[16]

While all caste and subcaste systems entail an element of role ascription, only in India are occupational categories so rigidly determined by heredity. In the Indian village we find subcastes (or outcastes) of sweepers, beggars, and even, in some instances, criminals and prostitutes. Such degrees of taxonomic nicety go well beyond the basic classification of the four *varnas*, namely the Brahmans (priests), the Kshatriyas (warriors), the Vaishyas (merchants), and the Sudras (artisans and laborers). This four-fold classification is understandable only in terms of the local context, for not all Brahmans act as priests (they may, for instance, be employed as cooks, for the food they prepare is ritually pure and thus acceptable to all other castes), and a Kshatriya is not forced to make his living by the sword. What is recognized in the community is subcaste membership, rather than the major caste divisions. As G. S. Ghurye points out, "Though it is the caste that is recognized by the society at large, it is the subcaste that is regarded by the particular caste and individual."[17]

As is well known, economic and technological development require an alteration of the occupational structure in that new tools require new skills, old skills become obsolete, and the fullest use must be made of the reservoir of talent. Furthermore, even relatively

---

tury," *The Annals of the American Academy of Political and Social Science* (National Character in the Perspective of the Social Sciences), Vol. 370, 1967, p. 128; Francis L. K. Hsu, *Clan, Caste, and Club*, New York, 1963; pp. 170–191.

[16] It should be added, though, that not all villages are made up of a multitude of castes and subcastes. Some are inhabited by a single caste. In multicomponent villages, the village *panchayat* should be distinguished from the caste or subcaste *panchayats*, bodies for intragroup control.

[17] G. S. Ghurye, *Caste and Class In India*, Bombay, 1959, p. 20.

gradual internal change will be hindered where occupational tasks are so thoroughly intertwined with ceremonial and social considerations as is the case in India. A skill learned in youth and reinforced by tradition will be known well, so well in fact that it constitutes a shackle to originality and experimentation. This is a particularly relevant consideration in understanding the problems of Indian agriculture. The country is unfortunate in that currently (1966) it is going through one of its periodic cycles of extreme drought, but it is doubtful whether even in "good years" India can now maintain itself at much above the harshest subsistence. Unless major improvements in agriculture are forthcoming—a task predicated on a major transformation in rural life and practices—it is certain that all the advances that India has made in other areas of national life and sectors of the economy will in the long run count for nothing.

To turn to other regions and problems, the Spanish-derived hierarchy of *castas* is relevant for an understanding of contemporary Latin America. In certain countries—Argentina, Chile, Uruguay, and Costa Rica—indigenous groups were either few in number or were rapidly annihilated in the first shock of conquest and colonization. As a result, the social structure of these lands evolved along the class lines of the settlers' Mediterranean homelands. The core area of caste culture (if we may so term it) in Latin America extends along the *cordillera* from northern Chile to central Mexico. In this region, the *conquistadores* established themselves as a ruling group over a sedentary native population of peasants, artisans, and originally, native elites. In due course, the Spaniards displaced the local aristocracy and the Indian or, where applicable, the Negro, became the lowest caste, while racial admixtures filled the intervening echelons.

Independence, which dates to the early decades of the nineteenth century, preserved the essentials of the colonial, political and social system, transferring power to locally-born aristocracies of Spanish descent. This rule by a European-derived elite has been aptly termed "internal colonialism,"[18] a condition that has resulted in the alienation of vast portions of the population from the national culture. The Indian villager remains economically peripheral. To the extent that he is dominated by, and owes social and economic obligations to, a *mestizo* hierarchy that controls the machinery of power, he may be said to participate in, but not be a member of, national life. This remains true even for those—such as plantation workers, miners, and

[18] See, for example, Pablo Gonzalez Casanova, "Internal Colonialism and National Development," *Studies in Comparative Development*, Vol. I, 1965, pp. 27–37.

much of the urban poor—who are more directly integrated into the national economy.

At the village level, a complex of relations and expectations constantly reinforces caste cleavages. While details vary from country to country and area to area, certain regularities in hierarchical relationships can be observed. Most obvious is the institutionalized subservience of the peasant, a combination of docility, lack of initiative, and accommodating stupidity. For the peasant to show originality and enterprise is calculated to engender the hostility of the ruling caste. What is demanded is a position of abject dependency. Conversely, the *ladino* or *mestizo* must constantly demonstrate his inherent superiority. Another facet of this *patron-peon* relationship is the stereotyped childishness of the Indian and the paternalism of the *mestizo*. While the peasant may resent his role, poverty forces compliance with the code. The traditional position of the American Negro, a product of similar circumstances, closely resembles that of the Latin American *peon*.

The roles of both the *mestizo* and the Indian are central to an understanding of the potentials and limitations of the Latin American village for technical change. The *mestizo* population avoids performing any tasks and exhibiting any behavior or attitude that may be associated with the menial caste. Considering that only this group has had the privilege of some degree of education, the situation is one in which potential talent cannot be fully utilized. Much of the work necessary for technical change involves the integration of manual activity with intellectual skills; the engineer unwilling to dirty his hands and the landlord who will not dismount from his horse can neither effectively learn nor transmit more advanced technology.

Apart from the obvious restraints imposed by poverty and inadequate education, the Indian peasant is bound by his traditional role of passivity. Initiative comes hard where the price of innovation can jeopardize a tenuous livelihood. The past-binding attitudes toward traditional techniques—the precipitate of generations of peasant life and labor—are reinforced by the fear of reprisals for deviating from expected behavior. Again, as in the case of southern European neofeudalism, the deviant faces both the rejection of his peers and the wrath of his overseers.

This is the pattern that has prevailed throughout much of the region under consideration. Some countries, such as Mexico, Venezuela, and Colombia, have progressed along the road to modernization. In these countries the caste barriers have been seriously weakened and steadily replaced by class-oriented structures. In Mexico, the genesis of this change must be dated to the Revolution of

1910 which, while it has had only peripheral impact on village technology, has played havoc with traditional social relations. In other lands, social and political changes are of more recent date and generally less pervasive.

The possibilities of change in class-based societies are chiefly limited to individual excursions up and down the class structure. In the long haul, major restructuring in class relationships can occur (a growth in the relative size and importance of a middle-class component, for example), but change and flexibility tend to be closely tied to individual, personal fortunes; it is not so much the structure that changes, but men's position within it. Caste-based societies are considerably more rigid. It is true that individual castes, more especially subcastes, can, in time, rise or fall in relative importance, but it is outside the caste structure, or following its dismantling, that opportunities present themselves for flexibility, for the talents and capacities of men to manifest themselves.

LINEAGE SYSTEMS

In contrast, clan-lineage systems constitute a much more flexible social structure, a structure characterized by inherent instability rather than by institutional rigidity. Lineages are composed of local groups organized on the basis of unilineal descent (patrilineal or matrilineal) whose members recognize the authority of generationally senior personages. Typically, they are grouped together into clans sharing a common identity, a common concept of kin membership, and tracing descent from an ancestral figure, real or fictive. Theoretically, the time perspective of the clan encompasses all descendants, living or dead, of the original founder. Lineages are of shallower depth—a few generations—and are based less on a general recognition of putative common ancestry than on the specific links of blood and marriage. Clans are exogamous and, needless to say, so are lineages.

What is distinctive of such structures is an ongoing evolutionary process whereby succeeding generations transform sublineages into lineages and lineages themselves rise and fall in relative importance. Without the tribal sphere—a confederation of clans—the same process is observable. In short, the hierarchy of lineages and clans tends to be fluid. A dynamic individual, the fortunes of war, the discontent of subordinate lineages and clans, all can operate to elevate a given corporate group or subdue one in a position of dominance. Commenting on Zulu social and political organization, Max Gluckman observes that:

A notable feature . . . throughout Zulu history is the creation of new groups as people move about, settled and increased, and the heads of all these groups were minor political officers who might in time achieve prominence. Since leadership was personal, these groups were not merely absorbed into existing political groups; their leaders became officers within the organization.

There was thus a constant creation of new officials which, with the rise in rank of brave warriors and wise men, permitted a high degree of social mobility. Any man, whatever his rank by birth, could become politically important if he had the ability, though those already established in high positions watched jealously over their rights and privileges.[19]

For such mobility it was not necessary—it was not even possible—for a man to desert his lineage or clan; rather, if he rose in status and power, his corporate group rose with him.

Lineage, clan, and tribal reshufflings could not and did not lead to anything approaching total control. Even the powerful Zulu kings were limited in their overlordship.

The king's position in the state was essentially his establishment in the "barrack area." He symbolized for the Zulu their identity as a nation as against the Swazi and other Bantu, and European Powers. The Nation was a federation of tribes whose separate identities were symbolized by their chiefs. The tribes were even autonomous within their national organization for on occasion many tribesmen supported their chiefs in quarrels with the king, though some were swayed by national loyalties.[20]

Within their respective, and more limited, spheres, the same may be said for clans and lineages.

Under the influence of a dominant individual, therefore, a relatively loose assemblage of clans might be brought to bear for common action, or even a federation of tribes organized into an instrument of power. Perhaps the historically most striking example of this phenomenon was the unification of Mongol tribes under the leadership of Jenghis Khan, a feat that for the space of two or three generations assured the Mongol army mastery over every battlefield. In the early nineteenth century, and with the aid of new military techniques, Shaka organized the Zulu into a unified kingdom capable of waging

[19] Max Gluckman, "The Kingdom of the Zulu of South Africa," *African Political Systems*, M. Fortes and E. E. Evans-Pritchard, eds., London, 1940, p. 45.
[20] Gluckman, *op. cit.*, p. 40.

war against the British. It must be stressed that in such cases much depends upon strong personal control—qualities of supreme leadership—and that generally a constant supply of plunder and tribute are prerequisites for internal cohesion. As the spacial boundaries of the system expand (through conquest and forced alliance), and the possibilities of plunder necessarily diminish, it can be expected that the forces of disintegration will come increasingly into play.

In part, this self-liquidating aspect of large political and social aggregates cobbled from clans and lineages is linked to the low level of technological development common to most clan-based societies. In short, few surpluses are offered for the erection of a permanent ruling class. Occupational roles are not highly specialized, and the lack of surpluses also prevents the establishment of urban centers and the development of elites separated from the agricultural population by different traditions and outlooks.[21]

LINEAGE SYSTEMS IN TRANSITION

Under certain circumstances, clan-lineage systems as the organizing principle for community life are likely to lose their political function. Apparently, the lineage systems of Archaic Greece were transformed into the *polis*, although the lineage per se still retained a residual importance in Classical Greek culture. In Southeast Asia, lineage-based societies were modified as they came under the influence of the centralized states of the lowland peoples. As a general rule, the evolution of a surplus economy has been detrimental to the survival of the lineage as a cohesive political force.

In recent times, the impact of colonial rule has been chiefly responsible for the political demise of lineage systems. Colonial administrators have generally found it expedient to elevate given local individuals as agents of the central power. Under these circumstances the corporate functions of the lineage and clan—to adjudicate disputes and organize production—are superseded by the organized coercive force of a colonial administration acting through its chosen

[21] Consequently, lineage systems are much more a tribal than a peasant phenomenon. It has, for instance, been questioned whether it is valid to speak of a sub-Saharan African peasantry prior to European colonization. See I. Schapera, "Economic Changes in South African Native Life," *Africa*, Vol. 1, 1928, pp. 170–188; L. A. Fallers, "Are African Cultivators to Be Called 'Peasants'?", *Current Anthropology*, Vol. II, April 1961.

representatives. The powers of the local agent, whether a traditional village functionary or an acculturated individual, were extended far beyond the bounds permitted by the traditional organization.

The individuals appointed to positions of authority by colonial officers—headmen, police boys, and "chiefs" of various categories—became progressively isolated from the population and came to constitute what is best described as a separate class of intermediaries. Stripped of local autonomy, the agricultural population increasingly took on the attributes of a true peasantry dependent upon larger political and economic entities.

With the emergence of independent states in former colonial areas, the trend toward a class structure has in no way abated. The new rulers have taken as their models the bureaucratic and administrative systems of the former metropolitan powers.

Lineage systems have proved remarkably adaptable to change within the limits imposed by their structure. Within the system there are few vested interests of an established type. The very fact that lineage-based societies are whole cultures does not lead to cleavages and conflicts over innovation or resistances to external stimuli. Despite nonstructural problems—no society being entirely "open" and all cultures being past-preserving—lineage systems, such as those in Africa and Oceania, have shown themselves highly receptive to a range of alien crops, ideas, and tools. Nevertheless, it should be understood that, for the most part, lineage systems, based as they are on simple technologies and a restricted corpus of knowledge, have an upward ceiling on the level of technology and organizational forms that they can absorb. Historically, therefore, such societies have commonly borrowed tools and techniques without the technological and intellectual infrastructure responsible for their development and production. It is also observable that, as technological diffusion and political and economic domination become more sustained, the lineage system as an organizing form is gradually transformed into either a class or caste system.

The peasant village and modern technology

Regardless of whether one is considering class-, caste-, or lineage-based societies, cultural resistance to technological change is seldom, if ever, total. Some important elements of modern technology have managed to penetrate village communities throughout the world. What is distinctive about these acquisitions is the characteristic of falling within the economic reach of the local population. Typically, this new technology can be used by single individuals or small groups and does not require initial major adjustments in the local social and economic structure.

The peasant village has absorbed technological components ranging from needles, knives, flashlights, matches, kerosene lamps, and transistor radios to buses, bicycles, and sewing machines. These imports have primed the population to accept more complex technology. Needless to say, not all such items (buses and trucks, for instance) are necessarily peasant owned or operated. Nevertheless, their impact on peasant life has been profound.

The itinerant stranger-trader has been an important agent of culture change and the diffusion of technologies and idea systems. This pattern is recognizable as early as the European Bronze Age and has comparable manifestations down to the present. In peasant villages the stranger-trader constituted a beneficial link with the national culture, introducing into peasant life the products of urban areas and, where applicable, foreign imports. Within recent memory, Mexican back country areas were chiefly serviced by *arrieros*, or muleteers, who carried a veritable cornucopia of articles such as cloth, needles, thread, household utensils, weapons, various condiments, and other articles requested on previous trips.[22]

The pack trader has been largely superseded in modern times by the locally domiciled merchant and the operator of tramp trucks. The impact on traditional society of the "mammy wagon" has been noted in many studies of West Africa. These vehicles combine imported chassis with locally made bodies to create a highly versatile form of transportation capable of carrying both goods and people. Like their predecessors, these traders fill in the nooks and crannies of the economy, freighting produce to and from isolated villages as well as main centers of commerce. By making manufactured goods more readily available and by extending the market for village produce, these entrepreneurs are facilitating a shift to more commercialized agriculture, and they are expanding the horizons of the local

[22] The itinerant trader also played a very important role in the opening of frontier parts of settled areas. In Western America, in South Africa, and in Australia the trader brought items that were vital to the maintenance of the frontier economy and that provided the edge of technological superiority over the indigenous inhabitants. See S. D. Neumark, *Economic Influences on the South African Frontier, 1652–1836*, Stanford, 1956, p. 4.

inhabitants. This type of transportation is the life-line of the local merchant and small-scale trader.

The small-scale trader or the street vendor performs the valuable function of breaking bulk and selling goods in small quantities within the economic compass of the peasant population and the urban poor. The figure of the street hawker or stall vendor selling a single cigarette, a handful of matches, a length of cloth, bread, tortillas, or a newspaper, cone of flour or sugar, or ladling a portion of cooking oil into a tin can, is commonplace in the streets and markets of the underdeveloped world. Equally evident is the individual preparing food over a charcoal grill for the village or urban workers and speciality items for the housewife.

Although the distinction between buses and trucks—especially those catering to peasant and out-of-the-way communities—is not firm in underdeveloped countries, the bus as a mover of people performs a unique function in the process of social and cultural change. The element of periodicity is more pronounced in buses and consequently permits the regular transportation of such things as staples, fresh produce, poultry, and pigs, together with their vendors. In regions with a tradition of regular market days, bus-line services have facilitated inter and intraregional contact of people and the exchange of goods. Also, the range of locally available commodities has been greatly expanded to include the products of other localities and industrially produced goods.

Quite apart from facilitating short distance contacts, the bus has linked the hinterlands to urban centers and, to a lesser degree, mines to plantations. The extraordinary growth of national capitals and other primary urban areas over the past few decades, which characterizes most of the underdeveloped world, can certainly be related in part to the availability of cheap bus transportation and familiarity with its use.

The urban migrant can make use of the same lines of communication to maintain ties with his natal village, a process that inevitably leads to the introduction of new ideas. Generally speaking, he brings back with him some industrial goods, new skills, and a modicum of cash sufficient to engage in new economic undertakings.

A range of relatively simple tools and machines have by now become fixtures in almost every peasant village. Perhaps most fundamental in their impact have been the sewing machine and the internal combustion engine in its various forms. Gasoline engines can be found grinding corn, pumping water, or crushing sugar cane, tasks that formerly required many hours of arduous toil by man or beast. In Mexican villages the motorized corn mill has revolutionized the housewife's daily routine. The peasant woman no longer spends the better part of the day tied to pestle and mortar grinding corn for the family's tortillas. Relieved of this traditional chore, she may now gather with her neighbors at the mill to chat and gossip while the corn is being ground.

Along the Nile, the creaking ox-powered *saqia* has since ancient times brought up water to irrigate the fields. In some localities gasoline pumps have replaced the *saqia* and expanded and improved agricultural production.

In contrast to other machine technologies, the sewing machine is equally a household article as it is a commercial one. In many parts of Asia and Africa the village tailor can be found in the streets or in his shop making clothes on order for the local peasants. In Latin America and Europe, where standards of living are for the most part higher, many a peasant family boasts its own sewing machine. With the aid of the sewing machine the peasant woman has been able to produce more clothing for her family and foster a demand for mass-produced textiles. The existence of cheap factory-made clothing as a basis for imitation, together with readily available mass-produced textiles, has led to the decline of regional styles of dress. While esthetically this trend may be regretted, it has a unifying effect on a nation by eliminating the symbolic barriers of regional attire.

Although not directly linked to production and transportation, the radio, particularly the transistor type, has certainly been a major agent of change in the peasant village. It has enhanced the peasant's awareness of the existence and happenings of the outside world, at both national and international levels. Radio advertising, for instance, has aided in the introduction of a wide range of new products, particularly packaged foodstuffs, and created markets of nationwide scope. More important is the fact that the peasant's political allegiance is being wooed through the medium of radio. Today, Radio Moscow, the Voice of America, Radio Peking, the B.B.C., and other important but more geographically restricted broadcasting stations (such as Radio Havana, Radio Cairo, and Radio Hanoi) all compete in the dissemination of gospels of change and betterment. Within their respective countries, governments seek to generate a spirit of national identity through radio communication. While it sometimes is difficult to gauge the response of the peasant to these many voices, the very fact that for the first time the peasant is called upon to judge between a variety of men, ideas, and institutions has nurtured the recognition that options are possible, poverty is remediable, and that man, by his own actions, can influence his destiny.

Bibliography

Anderson, R. T. and B. G. Anderson, *The Vanishing Village, a Danish Maritime Community*, Seattle, 1964.

Block, Marc, *French Rural History*, Berkeley and Los Angeles, 1966.

Block, Marc, *Feudal Society*, Volumes 1 and 2, Chicago, 1964.

Bourdieu, Pierre, *The Algerians*, Boston, 1962.

Brokensha, David W., *Social Change at Larteh, Ghana*, Oxford, 1966.

Burke, Fred G., *Local Government in Uganda*, Syracuse, 1964.

Dollard, John, *Caste and Class in a Southern Town*, New Haven, Conn., 1937.

Fraenkel, Merran, *Tribe and Class in Monrovia*, London, 1964.

Hammond, J. L. and Barbara, *The Town Labourer (1760–1832)*, London, 1917.

Hammond, J. L. and Barbara, *The Village Labourer*, London, 1911.

Hill, Polly, *Migrant Cocoa Farmers of Southern Ghana*, Cambridge, Eng., 1963.

Lewis, Oscar, *Village Life in Northern India*, New York, 1965.

Mitchell, J. Clyde, *Yao Village*, Manchester, 1956.

Reining, Conrad C., *The Zande Scheme*, Evanston, Ill., 1966.

van den Berghe, Pierre L., *Caneville: The Social Structure of a South African Town*, Middleton, Conn., 1964.

Wilson, Monica and Archie Mafeje, *Langa: A Study of Social Groups in an African Township*, Capetown, 1963.

V

❀

Urbanization, Education, and Development

URBANIZATION IN HISTORICAL PERSPECTIVE

Prior to the advent of European maritime expansion, urbanization in traditional societies was geared to the needs of administrative and religious control and in some degree to the requirements of trade. For the most part, such urban centers can be described best as "court cities," the seats of rulers, the centers of organized religion, and the habitations of all those who, in their various ways, met the personal needs and institutional requirements of native elites. In rudimentary state systems the exercise of power is concentrated in a limited number of urban centers (sometimes a single city), drawing tribute or taxation from the surrounding countryside. The urban elites, though small in number, frequently had at their disposal a substantial body of retainers and access to the products and services of other supporting groups. The instruments of power in the form of military forces and administrative and religious hierarchies, with lines of control radiating out to lower echelons, were positioned in the cities. Ancillary to the formal power structure were the urban artisans, traders, and a large class (or caste) of menials and slaves. While merchants can in origin be seen as tied to the demands of an aristocratic population, in later times commercial expansion widened the range of their activity and altered their social, and sometimes political status.

Some strategically located cities, such as ancient Alexandria or

Carthage, had a dominant trade orientation almost from their inception. Inevitably, such centers became politically powerful and sought to preserve and expand their economic dominance through territorial aggrandisement and, in some cases, maritime control. Conversely, the ancient city, by its very concentration of wealth, became a prime target for conquest, whether at the hands of rival city states or less settled peoples beyond the bounds of civilization. In many instances, the commercially oriented center, as a result of its own expansion and possible later conquest, eventually took on the attributes of a courtly city.

The maritime expansion of European civilization greatly changed court cities, both within Europe and in areas of European contact. National seats of power in Western Europe, Lisbon, Seville, and later Amsterdam and London, became administrative centers of far flung empires of trade and conquest. The industrial city was a later development and for the most part evolved in provincial localities somewhat removed from the traditional institutional structures.

Urbanization in colonial lands

Imperial conquest and induced colonial urbanization are phenomena with deep historical roots in both pre-Renaissance Europe and other areas of long-established political state systems. This situation can be documented in the case of Imperial Rome with its formal politics of using newly established urban centers as nuclei of Roman power; there are comparable cases in dynastic China. What is unique to the colonialism of post-Medieval Europe is the presence of technological developments—shipbuilding, cartography, and ordinance—that made imperialism possible on a global scale and in noncontiguous areas with vastly different cultural traditions.

The overseas colonial city replicated to a great extent the courtly city of the metropolitan land. Sometimes on a vast scale, at times in a much more reduced form, it served as an administrative center with its complement of vice-regal courts, garrisons, scribes, and ecclesiastical functionaries. In areas with long established urban life, such as the Orient, and the high culture areas of pre-Columbian America, colonial contact and conquest led to an expansion of urbanization and the establishment of the conquerors as a new elite caste. The racial and cultural differences that distinguished the new elite from the native inhabitants facilitated the formation of strongly differentiated caste structures. In some regions the expansion of trade that followed European maritime contact induced the creation of indigenous urban areas or the rise of European native entrepot cities. In West Africa, with the exception of Benin and some Yoruba towns, preconquest urbanization was a response to the opportunities of trade. Similarly, even prior to the advent of European conquest, a number of maritime Asian cities, Bombay and Canton, for example, had felt the stimulus of commerce.

In the densely settled areas of Asia the initial European conquest tended to be limited to a small number of strategic cities and small territorial enclaves. Later, with the spread of European power, major land masses came under political and military domination. While this consolidation entailed an increase in the expatriate population, the numbers involved never constituted more than a fraction of the total population. Larger proportionately, but still small in contrast to the overall native population, were those individuals and groups who for a variety of reasons identified with the colonizers. These ranged from princes, who found it expedient to side with the new military presence, to subordinate elements of the indigenous society, who sought to gain status through association.

The process of expansion inevitably called into being clerical personnel, primarily urban, to staff the lower echelons of the administration. In addition, the economic demands of chartered companies, commercial houses, and colonial administrations gave rise to a class of independent agents of officialdom, such as tax collectors and native contractors.

In less settled areas where alien penetration was more difficult, such as West Africa, the European population again was minimal. Forts and factories were established and staffed with European garrisons and a small body of traders and skilled personnel. The presence of these entities, plus the difficulties of expatriate recruitment, led to the training of selected local people in the skills necessary to maintain the enclave.

In other areas, such as parts of the Western Hemisphere where indigenous populations were large but not prohibitive to further settlement, European colonists were able to establish themselves in substantial numbers. While many of them settled in choice rural locations, the main focus of settlement was urban and resulted in the foundation of essentially European towns—the Spanish foundation towns of Mexico and the Andean altiplano—drawing their sustenance from a still largely Indian peasantry. Many of the class and caste distinctions that may be observed to the present day fall along the lines of this urban-rural dichotomy. Until recently, a structurally similar breakdown existed in former French North Africa.

Frequently in the colonial situation, the presence of an intrusive population, with its reserved residential sections, and the presence of a native population resulted in the formation of a dual city. The very names Old Delhi and New Delhi are a clear manifestation of this duality. While the nomenclature is not always as graphic, the lines of demarcation in such localities as Leopoldville and viceregal Mexico City were equally clear.

The class-caste structure that characterized colonial possessions has been perpetuated in a number of independent successor states. Elites trained in the traditions of the former governing power and sharing with the one-time dominant group many attributes of values and orientations have assumed political and administrative control. In the newly independent states of Africa and Asia the higher direction consists of a small fraction of the indigenous population strongly differentiated from the national masses by language, training, and standards of living. Functionaries, intellectuals and, in short, all who operate at a national level communicate in the language of the former colonial power, while the bulk of the population speaks a variety of native languages.

Elites and urbanization in developing areas

What is true of language is true of culture as a whole. These new elites are in the psychologically ambiguous position of exercizing leadership while at the same time operating in terms of the traditions and methods inherited from a colonial past. Lacking both the sanctions of traditional society and the coercive force backstopping the colonial regime, their position is precarious and national instability an ever-present danger. Their privileged position and the accumulation of wealth that often accompanies it make them obvious targets of discontent and revolutionary upheaval. Yet without the skills and knowledge that these elites monopolize, modernization and technical change will be difficult to achieve.

The problem in many underdeveloped countries is that of implementing justice for the population while at the same time restricting the personal privileges of elite groups and still assuring sufficient rewards so that their skills and training will contribute to the tasks of economic development.

In contrast to the former colonial regions of Asia and Africa, Latin American elites are not in the main descended from the indigenous population. While there was a substantial degree of racial admixture, the elites of the postindependence period were drawn primarily from European-derived sectors of the population. Three hundred years of colonial rule, together with a steady migration of settlers, assured that with independence the reins of power remained firmly in the hands of a creole aristocracy. The inflexibility of this ruling group constitutes one of the crucial problems of political stability and represents one of the major barriers to economic development and technological change.

Divorced from the masses of the population, the power structure of many underdeveloped nations depends on the military as an instrument of internal control. The military establishment in Latin America can be viewed as primarily an internal security force officered and led by individuals who are recruited from the upper echelons of society. Elsewhere, in former colonial areas, the military may have been drawn primarily from certain regions or tribes, a condition that poses added difficulty to civilian control. The military officers have frequently been trained in the military academies of the former colonial power and have acquired a greater identification with the West than have their civilian superiors. The conflict between pro-Western officers and radical civilian politicians has led to a number of military coups in the name of anticommunism or, conversely, a purge of the military. There are exceptions to this general pattern, especially, where power was handed over to traditional leaders, or where independence was a partial consequences of military strife. Also, in not a few cases the middle level officers (the proverbial young colonels) have been a revolutionary and nationalistic force.

Regardless of their political composition, the cost of maintaining military establishments is a heavy drain on resources. For Latin America the outlay is about 1.4 billion dollars per annum and purchases includes such sophisticated hardware as tanks, jets, and aircraft carriers. The prestige element is a strong motivating force.

EDUCATION AND URBANIZATION

As with their predecessors, the court city and the colonial city, the urban centers of underdeveloped nations contain most of the educated and technically trained talent of the country. In part, this distribution may be accounted for by the fact that it is primarily in the city that opportunities exist for the employment of sophisticated skills and personal economic advancement. Equal, if not more important, though, is the fact that virtually all of the educated people either have their roots in the city or have acquired a taste for the amenities and style of life peculiar to urban areas. These attitudes are strongly reinforced by the disdain that the middle and upper class city dwellers have for all manner of manual and mechanical tasks. Although these attitudes are by no means limited to the underdeveloped world, the caste aspects of urban-rural relationships, together with the great economic gulf that separates the well-to-do urbanite from the lowly countryman, fortify the desire for urban identity to a degree seldom found in more developed areas. It is not surprising, therefore, that governments and agencies of underdeveloped countries have encountered great difficulties in dislodging skilled and educated individuals from the urban matrix in order to staff posts in rural areas where they are critically needed.

Educational systems in underdeveloped countries evidence a strong urban bias. First of all, education at all levels is more accessible and of better quality in population centers; consequently, a disproportionate number of urbanites enjoy its benefits. Of greater significance, the content and structure of education has been greatly influenced by models, generally of European derivation, emphasizing classical subjects and traditional disciplines. In these educational institutions, law, medicine, philosophy, and letters all have an honored place not shared by engineering, agriculture, and science. Needless to say, this downgrading of scientific and technical education affects the rural areas and is detrimental to urban development as well.

Paradoxically, one of the problems facing underdeveloped countries with long-established systems of higher education, such as India and a number of Latin American countries, is the inability of the economy to absorb school graduates trained in traditional disciplines. While there is a crying need for the technologically trained, only a percentage of lawyers can ply their skills in the legal profession, while many are forced into semi-clerical positions where their training is only peripherally relevant. The same situation applies to graduates of literature and humanities departments and to many would-be social scientists. Such individuals may develop antipathies to a society that fails to recognize and reward their talents. This is especially true when education has been bought at the price of much personal sacrifice and effort in the expectation of delayed benefits.

Throughout all levels of the educational system in underdeveloped countries, the school dropout is both an economic and a social problem. Even a few years of schooling, while not sufficient to impart useful skills, generates a distaste for agricultural and manual labor. For the most part, these individuals swell the ranks of the urban unemployed or, when employed, each is discontented with his position, since it does not accord with his self-image. Discontent and disillusionment is even more prevalent in the case of those exposed to the heady atmosphere of university life. The "B.A. failed" in its many forms is a figure haunted by all the uncertainties of a marginal man who aspires to a social position that he can never achieve.

Education stripped of opportunity and partial education fostering a high self-evaluation with a low income are potent forces for revolutionary upheaval. This ferment can be a positive force for constructive change if it is directed toward necessary structural reforms in the society. Unfortunately, revolutions motivated by collective self-pity do not provide a firm base for social reconstruction. It is not surprising that in Karala, the Indian state with the highest level of literacy and with one of the least developed regional economies, the Communists have received over 40 percent of the electoral support, the highest proportion in India. Disaffected intellectuals and alienated members of the lower middle class can also form the nucleus of rightist reactions, as occurred in the Peronista movement in Argentina. The Fascist-Nazi phenomenon of the Europe of the 1920's and 1930's drew its strength in part from a similar well of discontent.

It is unfortunately true that there are many dysfunctional aspects to the educational structures of underdeveloped areas; this should not obscure the fact that education can be a vital force in economic development. An obvious basic need is a minimal level of education for the entire population. Even such rudimentary skills as literacy and simple arithmetic can unlock the doors of opportunity in societies where the social structure is relatively flexible and the economy affords suitable prospects for employment. Simple education can familiarize the population with ideas and concepts beyond their immediate experience and provide a propitious environment for continued learning and transformation.

In societies in the process of creating national educational systems, essentially *de novo* as is the case throughout most of Africa, even a modicum of education represents a significant economic advantage for the individual. Under these circumstances, where preconceptions on the character and use of education have not crystallized, the possibilities for the effective use of educational resources are enhanced. In much the same way, the loosening of traditional class and caste barriers brought about by internal political change, as in post-Revolutionary Mexico, can release previously dormant talents and open avenues for further educational advancement.

URBANIZATION AND THE EMERGENT MIDDLE CLASS

In some of the cities of the underdeveloped world what can best be referred to as a middle class is beginning to emerge. In part this phenomenon can be linked to a broadening of educational opportunities in urban areas. Unlike the historical situation in Europe, though, where the middle classes emerged along with evolving national state systems and later with mercantile expansion and industrialization, the middle classes of many underdeveloped areas have appeared prior to national independence and without being involved in major political and social changes. The European middle classes were in origin clearly distinguishable from the old aristocracies at one extreme and the peasants at the other. The very term "bourgeoisie" is indicative of a group who were town dwellers, intermediate in the social hierarchy, and primarily entrepreneurial in character. It is from within this group that the crown in the later Middle Ages and the Renaissance drew allies, financial support, and state servants for the tasks of national building and, later, overseas expansion. This identity as a separate class with an independent political and economic base has in some measure been retained to the present day.

Although middle class attitudes naturally varied from country to country, members of this class were, by and large, willing to engage in the pragmatic activities of government, commerce and, later, manufacturing. They were not loath to sit in the counting house, act as royal secretaries and ministers, or engage in trade—all activities that would have sullied the hands of the aristocracy. Furthermore, with the advent of industrialization many a middle class entrepreneur became intimately involved with machinery, modifying, inventing, and overseeing production. The rapid development of scientific agriculture from the Eighteenth Century onward—animal breeding, mechanization, crop rotation, and fertilization—owe much to the efforts of middle class gentlemen farmers.

The European middle classes were also instrumental in bringing about educational changes. Courtly and clerical education, which strongly emphasized metaphysics, logic, and dialectics, lacked the empirical and pragmatic qualities necessary for a commercial and industrial society. Consequently, the middle class was forced to create its own educational system, which, while not divorced from the classics and humanities, used the vernacular as the primary language of instruction and broadened the horizons of education to include technology and science. These new schools revamped the curricula, especially in the areas of history, geography, and mathematics.

The lines distinguishing the middle classes of the underdeveloped world are less clearly drawn than those characterizing the middle classes in their formative stages in Europe. The whole thrust of middle class development in Europe was in the direction of economic and administrative pursuits and the education and instruction necessary to carry them out. The aristocracy of Europe viewed wealth and the control of land primarily in terms of the maintenance of status and the preservation of tradition; wealth was a prerequisite of privilege. Given the belief that total production was fixed, then individual wealth could be increased solely at the expense of peasant welfare. For example, the increased demands for agricultural products in France during the seventeenth and eighteenth centuries led to a cycle of rent increases rather than to a major attempt to restructure agriculture and increase productivity. Needless to say, the peasantry were not pleased with the situation and, when in the course of time they found urban allies, the nobles felt their displeasure in 1789 and thereafter.[1]

The middle classes were willing to innovate in industrial and agricultural production. The economic world view that they developed stressed the possibilities of structural changes within an economic system and the concept that wealth was to be used for the creation of further wealth. These attitudes toward economic matters, together with the restrictions placed upon entry into the nobility, allow us to speak of a class-structured situation, with each class having its own recognized identity.

[1] Barrington Moore, Jr., *Social Origins of Dictatorship and Democracy: Lord and Peasant in the Making of the Modern World*, Boston, 1966, pp. 40–56.

MIDDLE CLASS VALUES IN DEVELOPING AREAS

The middle classes in the underdeveloped world, rather than being differentiated, seek in large measure to emulate the conditions and values of the established elites. In education much prestige accrues to those who pursue traditional educational goals. These aristocratic values toward education superimpose themselves, even in technical and applied professions. As a case in point, the universities established in British colonies tended to emulate the patterns of Oxbridge rather than those of the dissenting academies and red-brick universities. With independence and the greater recognized need for technical institutions, it is notable that such institutions and their graduates face the same discomforts born of class-consciousness and snobbery as do their counterparts in England. England, once the model of flexibility, is now paying the price for having taken the lead and shown the way. This aspiration for elite status among the middle class is also observable throughout much of Latin America, the former French dependencies, and most other areas of the underdeveloped world.

For these reasons it is often difficult to identify a functioning middle class in underdeveloped countries. In fact, the presence or absence of a middle class in specific underdeveloped countries is a matter of much debate among informed social scientists. Too frequently, it is assumed that the appearance of occupational groups duplicating middle class positions in the United States and other developed nations, is evidence of a middle class segment. Similarly, what in developed countries would be regarded as a middle-class standard of living—appliances, motor cars, and home ownership—is throughout most of the underdeveloped world a high style of life to which only the very rich can aspire. One has to take into consideration the economic condition of the masses of the population as being much more depressed, while the cost of consumer durables is often considerably higher in underdeveloped areas than in developed ones. Thus, for example, a standard American family car is transubstantiated, in countries like India, into a vehicle fit for an industrial magnate or a government minister.

It is certainly true that in some underdeveloped countries a middle class is in the process of emergence. However, the most notable examples of middle classes in Latin America and Asia—Argentina, Mexico, Japan, Brazil, and Chile—are encountered in lands that do not entirely fit the rubric of "underdeveloped." By any reasonable standard, Japan, with her well-established urban middle class, must be numbered among the developed nations. That in the course of one hundred years such a class has emerged indicates that even in previously very traditional societies the barriers to social transformation are not insurmountable. In Mexico it is possible, as some students have maintained, to trace the origins of the middle class deep into the nineteenth century. However, a middle class of substantial numbers, with a recognized identity and a significant share of political power, evolved as a consequence of the Mexican Revolution of 1910 and its aftermath. The stability of modern Mexico is in no small degree attributable to the integration of business men, political leaders, government employees, trade union officials, and professional people into a middle class component. Unfortunately, a number of factors, most important of which are a galloping population expansion and increased institutional rigidities, have caused some slowdown in Mexico's economic development. However, compared to most of her Latin neighbors, Mexico's economy must be considered healthy and progressive.

More pessimistic inferences can be drawn from the experiences of Brazil, Chile, and Argentina. At the turn of the century, Chile, Argentina, and the southeastern portion of Brazil were not far behind southern and eastern Europe in their economic and industrial development. While trailing considerably behind some of the developed continental countries, their booming economies and rich resources presaged a bountiful future, even perhaps a place among the first-rank nations. While all these countries have experienced internal political difficulties, and in some cases even minor international conflicts, none of these experiences can compare with the devastation that has twice ravaged Europe in this century; therefore, this factor cannot alone explain the twentieth century failure of these Latin American countries.

The brutal truth is that by and large the middle classes in these countries have failed to respond to the challenges of the twentieth century. Intellectually, they have been dominated by the economic ideas of the nineteenth century, while socially they have preferred to emulate the upper classes rather than forge an independent social consciousness. Furthermore, although they have enjoyed an important share of political power, it has generally been used (in conjunction with that of the upper classes) to preserve the established order. As a consequence, economic growth has been painfully slow, verging in fact on stagnation.

In some countries middle or upper level economic positions are, or were until recently, dominated by alien minorities lacking political power. The overseas Chinese in Southeast Asia, and to a lesser degree the Indians in former British East African and Southeast Asian colonies, are examples of this type. What is distinctive of this group is not only their foreign origin but also their lack of integration into the national culture. At times tolerated, or even encouraged, by ruling elites, the masses always regarded them as intrusive exploitative elements. Contemporary nationalism has made their position extremely precarious, as recent events in Southeast Asia and Kenya amply demonstrate.

Because of their marginal position in the political and social life of their countries of residence, it would be extreme to consider this element as constituting a normal middle class component. In nations where regionalism as well as tribalism is still strong, dominant social and economic groups from other parts of the country are in a position akin to the alien minorities described above. Their insecurity is exacerbated when their economic dominance is overwhelming and where regional disparities are marked. The slaughter and mass exodus of Ibos from the Northern Region of Nigeria indicate the depths of hatred and resentment that can be generated against those in strategic economic positions. With respect to former colonial areas, these middle level outsiders, whether from within or without the national borders, have borne the brunt of local hostility, since they experience a more continuous and direct contact with the local population than did colonial officials or the representatives of overseas trading houses. Furthermore, it often seems to local inhabitants that the trades and occupations dominated by these groups fall within their reasonable aspirations.

In effect, the middle classes of many underdeveloped countries are in reality so closely associated and aligned with the ruling elites that we can more meaningfully describe the total social structure as a two-class system. This observation is particularly true for sub-Saharan African where the combined middle and upper class is extremely small and, for the most part, of recent origin. To some degree the situation in Africa is atypical in that the upper colonial personnel have vacated their posts, creating a vacuum that has been filled by local power groups still very much in a state of flux.

Urbanization and the Working Class

Working classes in the modern sense should be distinguished from peasantry. While to a large extent recruited from the peasantry, the working class in underdeveloped countries is primarily located in urban centers. Where mining has been the major impetus for working class formation, a semi-urban situation tends to evolve. The local population is generally inadequate to meet the needs of extraction and processing, and consequently, labor is commonly drawn from a larger area, generally from diverse regional or tribal origins.

Full-time urban employment provides a new discipline for workers in that it forces them to rely on their wages to meet personal demands through the medium of a money economy. New urban working classes may, and often do, retain ties to the cultural groups and localities from which they originated. Nevertheless, life in the city creates new challenges that must be met with novel responses. Thus, while the worker may attempt to establish social relations patterned on rural kin and community models—what is sometimes referred to as the "urban village"—conditions of life in an urban setting restrict the scope of these associations. By definition, a large part of the worker's life must be led in a context alien to traditional rural society. This is particularly true of the worker's economic pursuits. Exposure to the external world is especially marked among men. Women for the most part remain at home, occupied in household work, and where employed tend to be domestics or follow localized service occupations, such as petty trading or taking in washing, ironing, or sewing.

Established working classes in underdeveloped countries tend in time to develop values, norms, and expectations that set them apart from both the peasantry and the middle and elite components of urban areas. While employment may be elsewhere in the city, the neighborhood forms the social focus for the urban worker and his family. Working class residential areas tend to be marked off into distinct neighborhoods which, in the scope of interpersonal relations, approximate that of the village. In part as a result of problems of urban overcrowding, neighborhoods tend to be inhabited with individuals from diverse rural origins. The rural carryover loses much of its particularism, and as a result, working class subcultures are derived from a more generalized form of the social structure of the countryside. In contrast to village identity, the worker recognizes more common ground with others in similar circumstances.

In the village, the individual is dependent upon various forms of kin relations for mutual aid and support. The new migrant to the city will seek out kin for orientation, residence, and assistance in obtaining employment. Once established, he makes contact with others outside his kin or village group and begins to weave a new set of social relations. Many of the functions performed by kin in the rural setting devolve upon voluntary associations in the city. While these voluntary associations may be tribal or village in origin (and even continue to retain superficial resemblances to rural forms), they quickly evolve new structures and recruit from a wider base. Typical of such associations and the needs they fulfill are burial, aid to the ill, and help in economic distress. This pattern is particularly marked in the growing cities of Africa and was a common feature of working class life in the emerging cities of the Industrial Revolution.

The working classes in Latin America are more atomistic. Functions performed by voluntary associations elsewhere are considered to be primarily family responsibilities or to fall within the purview of public or ecclesiastical charity. In India the caste system pervades the national culture, both urban and rural, and consequently, caste and subcaste associations can perform the same basic functions in both urban and rural setting.

URBANIZATION AND WORKING CLASS ORGANIZATION

The urban setting creates its own imperatives for collective action, which must be approached by new organizational forms. Most of these new organizational activities center around employment, particularly conflicts and problems between workers and employers. The trade union, in its various guises, is the main vehicle for collective interaction between employer and worker groups. Membership in a union, almost by definition, involves the worker in a broader range of social and political activities than was possible in the traditional setting. Though unions in underdeveloped countries tend to be weak, to achieve cohesion in only rare specific instances of strife, and to often be dominated by individuals who cannot be regarded as *bona fide* working class, even nominal participation in union affairs constitutes an affirmation of common purpose and interest. Regardless of the shortcomings of specific trade unions—bossism, corruption, and political manipulation—the resulting dissatisfaction and criticism indicate an awareness of putative union functions and the disparities between high ideals and actual practice.

Participation in union affairs entails a broadening of the individual's social, economic, and political perceptions. Political parties and movements are presented to him as offering avenues to personal and class betterment, stress is placed on the nation as an organic whole, while even the world outside the national borders is recognized as having some relevance to the individual's interests and the welfare of the nation. Frequently, a union will be aligned with, or subsidiary to, a political party or movement. If the party achieves political power, the union may find itself performing a semi-official function, either by legal enactment or political favor. Under these circumstances unions tend to lose much of their representative character and autonomy and become to some degree agents of governmental policy. Many unions are also aligned with international ideological, religious, or political movements. From these they may receive significant financial and organizational assistance, as do affiliates of the Catholic Action movement, International Confederation of Free Trade Unions (ICFTU) (a Western-oriented organization), and World Federation of Trade Unions (WFTU) (a Communist-aligned group).

As urbanization and industrialization proceed, political leaders are more prone to incorporate unions into the political structure. That governments in the contemporary world feel the necessity of appearing to have a popular base means that union participation, even as window dressing, validates the political power structure. Furthermore, central governments seek to create a national consciousness, which, given the conditions of urban life and industrialization, is best realized through appeals to the working class. Peasants, though numerically predominant, seldom provide a comparable alternative, as they are less susceptible to appeals and exhortations presented in terms of national goals and aspirations. Peasants, being geographically dispersed and locally oriented, have always been difficult to organize. In contrast, workers are strategically concentrated in cities and are thus more easily persuaded to participate in shows of national unity and political solidarity. A governmentally decreed day off from work, together with the efforts of official organizers, can do much to foster a massive turnout. Also, it must be stressed that the workers' strategic position in the cities, particularly in the national capital, allow them to exert a degree of leverage upon the government, which is beyond the capacity of the peasants. The failure of governments to respond to the more diffuse demands of the countryside is a source of much resentment and discontent among the peasants. Virtually everywhere the peasantry feels neglected, and rightly or wrongly, they assume that the benefits of modernization redound mainly on the inhabitants of urban areas.

In Africa and Asia unions were frequently a major force in independence movements. The union's demands for freedom of organization and improvement in economic conditions generally had the support of a large segment of the population, since their demands were mainly directed against expatriate enterprises and colonial governments. Because unions constituted the largest organized element of the working class population, and therefore provided a popular base for political and social action, they represented the natural allies of those elements in the professional and middle classes who were instrumental in achieving independence. Paradoxically, with independence, unions have dissipated much of their popular support and autonomy of action. Some of their ablest leaders have joined the ranks of government (sometimes at the highest level—for example, Tom Mboya and Sekou Touré) or been lured into managerial positions. Business enterprises, particularly those foreign based, have been forced to promote native personnel to managerial positions, a requirement that has been met by skimming unions of their top talent. That such a gambit coincidentally weakens union structure is not unnoted by governments and corporations. Whether the onetime militant occupies a desk in a ministry or a corporation front office, his ardor for working class causes is substantially cooled. Even outside the colonial sphere, long established revolutionary movements, as in the case of Mexico, evidence a similar phenomenon of "upward mobility."

As a general rule, union demands for higher wages and improved conditions are viewed by the peasants as being at their expense and by the government as a threat to internal stability and development plans. With independence there has also occurred a subtle shift in the orientation of those staffing the upper echelons of governments. Unions still receive preferred treatment, but one also finds a recognition that the problems of peasant agriculture must be solved, or at least alleviated, if the nation is to remain viable.

URBANIZATION AND THE CULTURE OF POVERTY

So far we have concerned ourselves with the established, steadily employed, and to some degree, organized urban worker. Important though this element is, due to its critical position in the economy and its relation to the overall political structure, it by no means forms the bulk of the lower urban classes. In fact, seen from below, a man with a decent paying factory job, or the even more prestigious public employee, or transport worker, enjoys a life of security and material comfort. The rapid growth of cities, primarily through migration from the countryside, has added greatly to the ranks of the lowest strata of urban life, often referred to as the disinherited proletariat, or more currently described as the culture of poverty. Perhaps the easiest way to understand this component is in terms of negatives or non-attributes. Severed from their rural cultural backgrounds, members of this underclass have not found a meaningful place in the community of the city. As a group they lack cohesion and organization, and their sense of hopelessness is pervasive. The educational opportunities that are sometimes available for their children are not utilized because the very futility of their condition prevents them from realizing that elevation is possible.

City life in underdeveloped countries is still very much dependent on the performance of a vast number of menial tasks. Street sweepers, porters and carriers, stevadors, night soilers, watchmen, shoeshine boys, newspaper sellers, servants of all kinds, and the myriad of menial office factotums, are all omnipresent in the city. For making a living in any of these occupations little more is needed than raw undifferentiated muscle power, the sole resource at the disposal of the lumpen proletariat. Unfortunately, even though there are many menial functions to be performed, the vast influx of population has made competition for them keen, pay pitifully inadequate, and security of tenure nonexistent. The vicissitudes of employment—the loss of job through sickness, a poor day's performance, and the capriciousness of the employer—are compounded by the seasonality of some menial urban jobs.

The instability of employment and the low income derived therefrom are among the major factors contributing to the social and personality characteristics of the culture of poverty. The personality syndromes of the culture of poverty are present in all situations where a combination of hopelessness in the face of genuine barriers to advancement rule the lives of individuals. Unstable family situations are ubiquitous due to families being the accidental outgrowth of conjugal relations that seldom acquire legal status. The paternal role is rarely viewed as binding; that the father may desert through any combination of job loss, the lure of a new partner, or simple boredom, compounds the instability. Consequently, to the extent that it is valid to speak of families at all, these revolve (if for no other reason than a biological one) around the mother. For children, the image of the father is naturally blurred, for it is filled by a succession of mates-of-the-moment. Products of such environments are anomic (they lack a sense of direction and values) and thoroughly ill-equipped to handle the complexities of urban life. Devoid of a blueprint for living, life is to be lived for the moment. Each experience is enjoyed in its own right without thought for the future. Drunkenness offers a cheap and rapid escape from the bleakness of reality and a momentary semblance of self-assertion. The sexual escapade offers many of the same possibilities. For the male it may represent his only form of conquest and triumph, while for the female it is her major weapon to lure, and hopefully control, the male. Needless to say, these conditions hardly make for a stable relationship. Home life offers little attraction for the male, so that even in semi-permanent unions the male is a stranger to his household and children. Even the city streets and the local tavern have more appeal than the miserable living quarters that are the lot of those disinherited. Stability in adult social relations is structured along sexual lines; men choose companions for drinking, bragging, and rough-housing, while women associate with female neighbors and kin for mutual aid and gossip.

The conditions that we have outlined tend to perpetuate themselves, for those born in them are instilled with the attributes of their progenitors and peers. This continuation over time of attitudinal and behavioral patterns is what permits us to speak of this phenomenon as a "culture" of poverty. It should be understood, though, that poverty is but one of the discrete features of this life. Economic poverty alone does not automatically constitute social disorganization and personal normlessness; rather, what is involved is a kind of poverty of the spirit. To paraphrase Hobbes, life in the culture of poverty is solitary, poor, nasty, brutish, and short.

There are two further factors that help to perpetuate the culture of poverty. Like all other groups, its members apply boundary-maintaining mechanisms; an individual attempting to break out is fair game for ridicule and hostility—after all, who does he think he is? The society at large surveying the situation focuses on the overt manifestations of poverty: filth, ignorance, lack of initiative, looseness of morals, and unreliability. These conditions are regarded almost as inherent in the baser elements of society, and as a result, little attempt is made to remedy the situation. Employers and officials expect unreliability and, naturally, unreliability is forthcoming.

URBANIZATION AND POPULATION PROBLEMS

The massive run on the cities, which has characterized demographic patterns in the underdeveloped world over the past three or four decades, and increasingly since the Second World War, has fed those sectors of the population generally subsumed under the culture of poverty. One effect of this trend has been to add to the cost of social services—minimal though they may be—which are vastly more expensive in the cities than in rural areas. Cities are plagued with masses of the unemployed and underemployed who can contribute little to economic development. While the rigid preconceptions of upper class elements about the inherent inferiority of the poor are not based on a rational analysis of the problem, the optimism of many local and foreign economists and politicians concerning the developmental possibilities of an abundant pool of labor is equally unjustifiable. In a survey of Latin American attitudes toward problems of population growth, J. Mayone Stycos quotes, as a typical statement of the "pronatalist" position, *El Tiempo* of Bogotá, to the effect that:

Despite its demographic evolution, Latin America does not face an immediate threat of over-population, since it has approximately a seventh part of the earth's surface, and only a tenth of its population.[2]

While economists are generally more cautious in their appraisals of the problems of population growth, they nevertheless view existing labor surpluses as an abundant factor of production for industrialization. Underlying this assumption is the belief that in developing economies labor-intensive processes are more suited to local conditions. It is certainly true that traditional productive processes, whether agricultural or craft, use proportionately more labor than capital; however, this is both the cause and the result of underdevelopment. What is seldom recognized is that a modern industrial base cannot be erected on the foundation of an untutored multitude. Phrased differently, the clock of technology cannot readily be turned back without saddling underdeveloped countries with obsolete enterprises. As a general rule, capital-intensive techniques are the ones embodying the latest scientific and technological achievements. Thus, we

[2] J. Mayone Stycos, "Opinions of Latin-American Intellectuals on Population Problems and Birth Control," *The Annals of the American Academy of Political and Social Science*, Vol. 360, 1965, p. 14.

often find that a capital-intensive technique economizes both in the use of *labor* and the use of *capital*.[3] Too often, labor-intensive industries are protected by high tariffs, which raises the price of goods on the domestic market. The consumers are forced to pay a disguised tax in the form of higher prices for what more often than not turn out to be goods of low quality. Often the cost of national prestige industries is borne by those least able to cope with it.

Labor in a technological environment

Modern technological processes require industrial habits of mind. The "unskilled" operative of developed countries is a product of an unconscious cultural conditioning. He takes for granted basic ideas of cause and effect and mechanical process. The environment in which he is brought up is one in which advanced technology, in both sophisticated and simple forms, is omnipresent. Even without formal training, the individual becomes attuned to his environment by the very fact of being present in it. All cultures have such unconscious learning, and each child is exposed to it from a very early age.

The child raised in a technological society acquires a familiarity to a mechanistic world and, one might almost say, a rudimentary understanding of the basic principles of scientific causation. It is true that some parents seek to reinforce this learning process consciously, by providing their children with specifically designed "creative" and scientific toys. However, since toys in all cultures are a microcosm of the adult world, toys and play activities are part of the informal learning process without specific intent. Formal educational systems greatly expand this scope of understanding, but they are at the same time predicated upon it.

Any instructional system automatically assumes a common cultural background of learning experience. An instructional system, or, for that matter, any component of culture, when removed from its context and introduced into another cultural environment, encounters difficulties of adjustment.

To people raised in the culture of poverty, or in fact to the majority of inhabitants in underdeveloped countries, a broad range

[3] Benjamin Higgins, *Economic Development*, New York, 1959, pp. 672–673.

of technological experience is alien. The basic industrial habits of mind necessary to operate a modern technological enterprise must be learned *in toto*, often at a relatively advanced age. In other words, what is informally learned in one culture must be formally learned in another.

Problems may arise, though, when formal education and training conflict with deeply held values and different world views. As experience in underdeveloped countries shows, industrial habits of mind and the behavior necessary for technological society are hard to instill. Formal training is useful and bridges part of the gap, but as the low level of labor productivity and the poor quality of goods indicate, a relatively long period of acquaintanceship and experience is needed to acquire mastery of industrial technology. It should not be assumed that these failings are restricted to the working classes.

Comparable to the shortcomings in the labor force, there often is a less than complete understanding of modern techniques by managerial and professional personnel. These difficulties are compounded when expatriate teachers or managers fail to recognize the informal aspects of their own upbringing. When the local trainees or students do not meet the expectations of overseas supervisors, they are often stereotyped as being congenitally stupid, immature ("boys"), or shiftless.

EDUCATION AND TECHNICAL CHANGE

As the formative years of life are all important, the value of a system of universal education cannot be exaggerated. Initially, a school program has to overcome the cultural inertia and the scientific and technological shortcomings of the social environment. Nevertheless, if changes of a nonreversible nature in a social system are to take place, education must constitute the primary force for transformation. Even in the most traditional societies children represent the most flexible element. The critical factor often reduces itself to the provision of teachers, not only competent in their subjects, but also able to work constructively within the restraints of environments that may be alien to them. This pedagogic problem covers not only expatriate instructors but also those nationals teaching children of different classes or cultural origins.

Some forms of education have an immediate impact. Elementary skills or agricultural techniques may be directly applied to raising standards of living. This aspect of education, while certainly very important in underdeveloped countries, has but limited benefits. It does not provide an adequate foundation for the further intellectual development of the individual. What is needed in underdeveloped countries is not simply an understanding of techniques, but also a comprehension of the underlying basic principles and methods of inquiry. Pure technique learning is not conducive to the dynamic integration of knowledge and its application to problem solving at any level.

Bibliography

Ashby, Eric, *Technology and the Academics*, New York, 1959.

Banton, Michael, *West African City*, London, 1957.

Cipolla, Carlo M., *Guns and Sails*, London, 1965.

Davies, Ioan, *African Trade Unions*, Hammondsworth, Eng., 1966.

De Gregori, Thomas, *Technology and the Economic Development of the Tropical African Frontier*, Cleveland, 1968.

Elkan, Walter, *Migrants and Proletarians*, London, 1960.

Epstein, A. L., *Politics in an Urban African Community*, Manchester, 1958.

Ginzberg, Eli and Herbert Smith, *Manpower Strategy for Developing Countries: Lessons from Ethiopia*, New York, 1967.

Hanson, John W. and Cole S. Brembeck (eds.), *Education and the Development of Nations*, New York, 1966.

Hellman, Ellen, *Sellgoods: A Sociological Survey of an African Commercial Labour Force*, Johannesburg, 1953.

Leslie, J. A. K., *A Survey of Dar-es-Salaam*, London, 1963.

Lewis, Oscar, *The Children of Sanchez*, New York, 1961.

Lewis, Oscar, *La Vida*, New York, 1966.

Little, Kenneth, *West African Urbanization: A Study of Voluntary Association in Social Change*, Cambridge, Eng., 1965.

Mantoux, P., *The Industrial Revolution in the Eighteenth Century*, New York, 1961.

Mitchell, J. Clyde, *Sociological Background to African Labour*, Salisbury, 1961.

Onyemelukwe, C. C., *Problems of Industrial Planning and Management in Nigeria*, New York, 1966.

Parry, J. H., *The Age of Reconnaissance*, New York, 1963.

Pirenne, Henri, *Medieval Cities*, New York, 1956.

Pi-Sunyer, Oriol, *Zamora: A Regional Economy in Mexico*, New Orleans, 1967.

Scott, Roger, *The Development of Trade Unions in Uganda*, Nairobi, 1966.

Sjoberg, Gideon, *The Pre-Industrial City*, Glencoe, Ill., 1961.

Whiteford, Andrew H., *Two Cities of Latin America*, New York, 1964.

VI

Development Planning

TECHNOLOGY AND CAPITAL THEORY

Development planning involves the organization of human activity toward the maximization of economic performance consistent with other social and political objectives. A variety of theories attempts to explain the manner in which economic growth occurs. Since economic activity is but part of a broader behavioral complex, the implementation of a development plan demands an understanding of the motivations of the population and the way in which it is likely to respond to incentives, exhortations, and directions.

Traditional growth theories center on savings and capital formation. Since the 1930's, due in large part to the influence of Keynes, the automatic utilization of savings has been questioned. More recently, there are indications that technological change is a more important factor in the stimulation of economic growth than capital accumulation.

In their monumental study of British economic growth, Dean and Cole find no evidence that the early stages of the Industrial Revolution were accompanied by an increase in the rate of saving.[1] There occurred in the 1700's, however, a series of important inventions, which initiated a radical transformation of the British economy.

[1] Dean and W. A. Cole, *British Economic Growth 1688–1959*, Cambridge, Eng., 1962, pp. 259–262, 303–334.

Many of these inventions and developments—canals and turnpikes, the spinning jenny—actually economized on the use of capital. Efficient transportation reduced the amount of capital tied up in inventories. Similarly, in the textile industry the jenny and related inventions increased labor productivity, compensating in part, at least, for the increased capital costs of the equipment. In an equally exhaustive study of the early periods of industrialization of other countries, Simon Kuznets does not find an overall correlation between rate of saving and acceleration of economic growth. In fact, in some countries there was actually a decline in relative capital formation.[2] As S. H. Frankel has noted, not only do many new inventions require no increase in capital, but "they may wipe capital out and are all the more beneficent for thus enabling us to discard the tools, machinery, and stock rendered unnecessary"[3] by new methods of production.

In recent years, there have been a number of historical statistical studies attempting to ascertain the relative importance of capital formation and technological change in economic growth. Admittedly, there are many difficulties in this type of quantitative analysis, but the general thrust of these studies indicates that only 15 to 20 percent of increased per capita income can be attributed to a rise in capital formation. The rest of the increment in per capita income is generally accounted for by some form of technological change, including improvements in organization and education.[4]

In underdeveloped countries, while the quantity of capital is important, particularly foreign exchange, the critical problem is how available savings are used. As M. M. Postan has noted for England, "There were enough rich people in the country to finance an economic effort far in excess of the modest activities of the leaders of the Industrial Revolution."[5] Considering the amount of dead wealth present

[2] Simon Kuznets, "Quantitative Aspects of Economic Growth: Part VI—Long Term Trends in Capital Formation Proportions," *Economic Development and Culture Change*, Vol. IX, No. 4, Part 2, 19, p. 12.

[3] S. H. Frankel, "Capital and Capital Supply in Relation to the Development of Africa," in E. A. G. Robinson (ed.), *Economic Development for Africa South of the Sahara*, London, 1964, p. 417.

[4] See, for example, Robert Solow, "Technical Change and Aggregate Production Function," *Review of Economics and Statistics*, Vol. 39, No. 3, 19; Moses Abramovitz, "Resource Output Trends in the U.S. since 1870," *American Economic Review*, Vol. 46, No. 2, 19; Solomon Fabricant, *Economic Progress and Economic Change*, New York, 1954; and John W. Kendrick, *Productivity Trends in the United States*, Princeton, N.J., 1961.

[5] M. M. Postan, "The Accumulation of Capital," *Economic History Review*, Vol. VI, 1935, p. 2.

in many underdeveloped countries—numbered accounts in Swiss banks, foreign exchange potential in gold and jewelry, and accumulated public foreign exchange holdings—Postan's observation has a great deal of contemporary relevance. Historically, countries that followed England's lead in industrialization tended to generate economic development with their own resources. This is true not only for Western economies but also for such nations as Russia and Japan.

FINANCE AND THE PROBLEMS OF DEVELOPMENT

Although the historical analogy can illuminate, it can also obscure. The underdeveloped countries of today are in many ways in a different position than were their precursors. There are both advantages and disadvantages to being a late starter. On the positive side, all the accumulated knowledge of the developed world creates a potential for more rapid advance. Negatively, the higher foreign exchange costs of a modern technology, which cannot easily be developed internally, and the dependency relationship that many underdeveloped countries find themselves in, serve to perpetuate a condition of economic backwardness. The dependency element may be a more critical factor in that a number of underdeveloped countries have been net exporters of savings and financial resources. For instance, the dependencies of British Colonial Africa down to the mid-fifties (and in some cases after independence) transferred savings through the banking system to metropolitan banks because suitable domestic outlets for investment were not available.[6] The banker's canons of financial soundness may have been overly conservative and culture-bound; despite this factor, a genuine lack of "absorbtive capacity" must be recognized.

If local financial resources are not utilized, it is not surprising that many foreign aid programs have failed. Some foreign aid has gone to swell the bank accounts of political potentates and expand local

[6] W. T. Newlyn and D. C. Rowan, *Money and Banking in British Colonial Africa*, Oxford, 1954. For an overall view of the outward flow of financial resources from British Colonial Africa to England, see Thomas R. De Gregori, *Technology and the Economic Development of the Tropical African Frontier*, Cleveland, Ohio, 1968, Chapters VI to X; and for a general comment on the flow of financial and real resources, see W. C. Gordon, "Foreign Investment," Special Issue of *The Business Review*, Houston, Fall 1962, Vol. 9.

bureaucracies. Even so, foreign business enterprise frequently finds opportunities for investment. Where local funds are idle or expatriated, the critical foreign contribution is not financial but technological and organizational. In Venezuela, for instance, the introduction of supermarkets had to await the organizational skills of Nelson Rockefeller, although financially such enterprises fell well within the capacity of local men of wealth.

Given that the main contribution of foreign enterprises lies in the skills that they have at their disposal, it is questionable whether it is wise for an underdeveloped country to encourage foreign capital investment as a general policy. If the skills and know-how can be purchased, as is frequently the case, this represents an alternative that allows the country to keep a certain amount of control over its economic destiny and does not place a long-term burden on its foreign exchange for debt service and profit repatriation. Obviously, this option is predicated on the marshaling of idle foreign exchange resources. Pemex, the Mexican government oil monopoly, regularly subcontracts geological prospecting to American oil companies. Kaiser Industries has found it quite profitable to provide a variety of technological services, either through outright sale or through a variety of organizational forms falling considerably short of outright ownership. Japan has established a strong historical precedent for using her own financial resources in combination with foreign technology and experience. It is interesting to note that Japan today is a major exporter of industrial expertise. Similarly, some of the smaller countries with a pool of technical resources, such as Israel and Italy, have made an impact in the underdeveloped world by giving or selling aid and technical services. This success must in part be attributed to the fact that these countries by necessity operate at a scale congruent with the technological needs of the recipient countries. Furthermore, neither Israel nor Italy is in a position to dominate a foreign economy, and consequently, fears of external domination are assuaged.

EXPORT STRUCTURES AND THE PROBLEMS OF DEVELOPMENT

In contrast to the nineteenth century, contemporary underdeveloped countries are burdened with the problems of economies structured to meet the requirements of a small group of privileged nations. Typically, these nations derive their foreign exchange primarily from the sale of a limited number of raw materials or commodities such as oil, copper, sugar, cacao, and bananas. Being closely tied to the market demands of industrial countries, these raw commodity-producing economies are especially subject to detrimental external influences. Synthetics, for instance, represent a major threat, as does product substitution by other raw commodities. Synthetic fibers and synthetic rubber, while not causing an absolute decline in world demand for the natural products, have nevertheless slowed their rates of growth. Stainless steel and aluminum have in recent years become important substitutes for chrome. Some minor products, which were important to the producing countries—for instance, curare, vanilla, and cochineal—have been virtually superseded by substitutes. Chilean saltpetre, while it still finds a place as fertilizer in the world economy, has lost its preeminence as a nitrate component in the manufacture of explosives. Sugar, once the basis of prosperity for many Caribbean lands, has suffered from serious competition by sugar-beet, as well as from the diffusion of sugar cane cultivation to many other tropical and subtropical areas.

Sugar-beet would not be a major competitor with cane sugar except for the protectionist policies of industrial countries that have fostered its development for strategic and other reasons.

Sugar exemplifies the complaints of underdeveloped countries that industrial nations, by tariff protection and subsidy, have fostered inefficient production of substitutes when such a policy is in their interests.[7] It should not be forgotten that the largest raw commodity producers are still the industrial countries—especially the large ones —and that in the majority of cases, they are also the most efficient producers of raw commodities. Consequently, where these governments elect, for whatever reason, to encourage inefficient commodity production, or stimulate expansion in more efficient areas, such a

[7] The usual result of such policies is a rise in the price of the product for the consumer in industrialized countries and a drop in both the quantity exported by underdeveloped lands and the profits derived from such exports. The difference between production costs and high sale prices is mostly taken up in the tariffs levied by the importing country. The U.S. sugar policy is an exception to most such cases in that while it raises the price of the commodity to the American consumer, the higher domestic price is paid to selected external suppliers who are allowed a Congressionally determined quota of the market. The special case of sugar must be understood in terms of the historic and economic relationships that exist between the United States and the Latin American and Caribbean republics.

policy can seriously affect the economies of the underdeveloped world. If developed countries choose to discriminate in their purchase of commodities in excess supply, this offers them an important political lever not available to the underdeveloped.

RAW COMMODITY EXPORTS

Many underdeveloped countries fall within the tropical and semitropical climatic ranges. There is therefore a considerable degree of overlap in agricultural potential which, in the long run, has worked to the detriment of these countries. Nations that have developed exports based upon agricultural commodities have frequently, and sometimes suddenly, faced stiff or ruinous competition from lands with similar climatic endowments. To this must be added the circumstance of colonialism where metropolitan powers considered it necessary to have a full range of tropical products produced in their overseas dependencies, even at the price of economic inefficiency. Of course, sometimes this goal of imperial self-sufficiency has proved highly beneficial to a colony, as is amply demonstrated in the cases of rubber in Malaya and cotton in British Africa.

Imperial self-sufficiency has given way to diversification of independent national economies. As a policy it has many advantages: it may function as a hedge against natural disasters affecting one crop, or offset a price drop in a major commodity export. Diversification may also result in a saving on transportation and foreign exchange. However, frequently the new production is inefficient and must be protected from external competition; consequently, it places an additional burden on the local consumer and deprives a fellow underdeveloped country of a portion of its market. Where the production is efficient, it may merely add to a glutted market, a condition that brings loud cries of protest from other nations of the underdeveloped world.

A hazard that faces any country heavily dependent on exports is the possibility that a competitor, through more efficient techniques of production and distribution, will deprive it of a portion of its overseas market. This circumstance is by no means limited to underdeveloped countries, as is evident in the case of Great Britain, which, beginning in the 1870's, steadily lost her preeminent position as the workshop of the world.

The dangers of market loss nevertheless constitute a greater threat to underdeveloped countries heavily dependent on a limited range of agricultural crops. Environmental limitations, when added to historical patterns of production and export, preclude rapid and relatively painless adjustments. Brazil is the classic case of a country whose exports have suffered from the onslaughts of competition. At one time or another she has been the major—if not the near monopoly—supplier of sugar, rubber, and coffee. During the colonial period and well into independence, the sugar provinces of Northeastern Brazil dominated the national economy. At a later date, with the increased demand for rubber following the development of the vulcanization process, the natural rubber resources of the Amazon valley provided a swift ascent to affluence for a portion of the Brazilian population and led to the grandiose booming of a number of riverine cities. This temporary opulence was paid for by the virtual enslavement of the native inhabitants of the easily tapped regions of the Amazon drainage and an accompanying decline in their number. Those who managed to escape the lash of the overseers sought refuge in the interior forests. Paralleling this abuse of the native population was the indiscriminate tapping of rubber trees: initial high production was achieved at the expense of future output. A more important factor in economic decline, however, was the introduction of *Havea brazilensis* into British Malaya at the turn of the century and its rapid establishment as a plantation crop. Although attempts have been made to institute plantation production in the Amazon area, rubber has never proved so successful in Brazil as in the Far East and, more recently, in Africa. In fact, the sugar and rubber regions of Brazil are now poverty stricken and a source of national concern.

Coffee is grown in Southeastern Brazil, chiefly in the state of São Paulo. Until recent times, Brazilian coffee dominated the international market. During the 1930's, Brazil's attempt to counter the effects of the great depression by withholding part of the crop allowed Colombia and other countries to capture a segment of her market. Since World War II, a large number of African and Latin American nations have become significant producers. The increased use of lowland beans for soluble or instant coffee has created a shift in market demand favoring these previously less well-regarded varieties and the countries that produce them. Brazil remains the largest exporter of coffee, but her preeminence is becoming increasingly challenged by recent entrants into the market.

RAW COMMODITIES: THE PROBLEM OF PRICE STABILITY

A major concern of the raw commodity exporting countries is the adversely changing terms of trade since the end of the Korean War.[8] From the end of World War II to the mid-fifties, prices rose rapidly as a consequence of pent-up war demands and the boom conditions and stock-piling of the Korean period. Commodity producers responded to the higher prices with increased production. From 1954 onwards, the continued expansion in production and slackening of demand reversed the price trends for most commodities and in some cases created unmanageable surpluses. This distressing situation can be partially accounted for by the carry-over from the peak demand periods during which new areas were opened and crops brought under cultivation, and previously uneconomic mineral deposits were exploited. Furthermore, in the face of falling prices, the response of individual countries was not to cut back production but rather to maintain or increase existing levels in an attempt to gain a larger share of the international market. Attempts at international commodity agreements have not proved too successful. These agreements are not binding, and national interest being always paramount, if a country feels overly constrained it has the option of breaking an agreement and dumping its commodities on the open market. Also, agreements are hard to police and, of course, there are some countries that do not subscribe to them.

The generalizations of the preceding paragraphs find support in the available statistics. As to the dependence of underdeveloped countries on one or two export crops, a study by the Stanford Research Institute shows that of twenty-six countries surveyed, fifteen overwhelmingly depended upon the sale of coffee, tea, or cocoa for their foreign exchange.[9] While the demand for these commodities in

[8] Currently, there is some controversy among professional economists and statisticians as to whether or not price fluctuations are greater for underdeveloped countries and whether the *long-term* trend of the terms of trade is in fact adverse for underdeveloped countries. The available data certainly leave room for different interpretations; however, it cannot be denied as a psychological fact that leaders of underdeveloped countries believe in this adverse trend, and their economic policies are fashioned accordingly. Furthermore, while aggregate figures admit of different interpretations, it is clear that some countries have experienced throughout the last decade serious price declines for their exports and equally marked rising prices for their imports.

[9] Stanford Research Institute, "Possible Non-Military Scientific Develop-

developed countries has continued to rise, it has done so very slowly and chiefly in relation to population growth. Where a substantial level of affluence has already been achieved, such minor items in the household budget are unlikely to be responsive to downward price movements. On the other hand, sudden and substantial price increases are frequently viewed as outrageous by the purchasers, and consumer resistance stiffens. It is a frequently observed fact that the increased coffee prices of the early fifties resulted in a shift in consumer tastes and a marked preference by the American coffee drinker for a weaker brew. At the same time, tea was making inroads into the traditional beverage habits of the American public. Furthermore, as far as the American coffee market is concerned, downward price movements have not generated much increased demand. It is also questionable whether many of the benefits of a lower commodity price are passed on to the consumer.

RAW COMMODITIES: MARKET POTENTIALS

There are, however, a number of developed countries that do hold substantial promise for market expansion. In the Soviet Union and Eastern Europe per capita consumption of cocoa and coffee is very low. In the early sixties, per capita consumption of coffee was below 200 grams, a figure that does not begin to approach the 4000 to 8000 grams-level of many Western countries.[10] It is to be expected that rising consumer pressures will substantially elevate the imports of these products. Some central European countries—Czechoslovakia in particular—have a pre-World War II tradition of processing and consuming cocoa products. It is also apparent that present low levels of consumption reflect government policy rather than consumer preference. Even the Soviet Union's recent close economic relation with the world's largest cocoa producer, Ghana, did not result in an appreciable rise in domestic cocoa consumption. In fact, there have

---

ments and Their Potential Impact on Foreign Policy Problems of the United States," *U.S. Foreign Policy Compilation of Studies*, No. 2, September 1959, Washington, D.C., 1961, pp. 93–198.

[10] Proceedings of the United Nations Conference on Trade and Development (Geneva, 23 March–16 June, 1964), Vol. 3, *Commodity Trade*, New York, 1964, p. 310.

been frequent charges that the Soviet Union was reexporting ("dumping") to traditional Western European markets at a critical time (1965–1966) when cocoa producers were attempting to raise prices by restricting exports.

Japan holds similar promise as a country that is experiencing rapid economic growth and changes in consumer taste. Since World War II, the "Westernization" of Japanese consumer patterns has resulted in an increased demand for raw commodities such as cocoa and coffee. One manifestation of this phenomenon has been the establishment of espresso-type coffee houses in Japanese urban areas. The increasing consumption in cocoa products is shown by the 300 percent increase in cocoa imports from 1958 to 1964.[11] This potential is not unrecognized. A number of African countries, such as Uganda and Nigeria, import manufactured goods from Japan far in excess of the value of their commodity exports to Japan. These countries are trying, by bilateral agreement and other means, to encourage Japan to purchase a greater quantity of their exports.

Other commodities, while having market problems of different kinds, nevertheless have experienced price difficulties comparable to those outlined for coffee, tea, and cocoa. It should be noted, however, that, difficult as the price situation may have been in the post-Korean War boom, few if any commodities have experienced price fluctuations as severe as those of the period between the world wars. Yet, fluctuations still resulted in instability in export proceeds and a consequent difficulty in making planned expenditures for development. According to the findings of the United Nations Food and Agriculture Organization (FAO), the underdeveloped countries lost nearly 600 million dollars as a result of price declines between 1955–1959. This sum was 60 percent greater than the total foreign aid to these countries from all sources. Many underdeveloped countries in fact claim that, while they have experienced growth in terms of total production, this increase has been offset, or more than offset, by downward price movements. This has been true particularly for the food and beverage products discussed previously—which are, after all, peripheral to consumer needs—but it is also valid for more stable commodities such as cotton.

The increase in the volume of world exports of a little over a quarter between 1953–55 and 1959–61 was entirely offset by the decline in prices, so that the value of world exports remained unchanged at $2,300 million.[12]

[11] U.N., *op. cit.*, p. 311.
[12] U.N., *op. cit.*, p. 321.

It is now generally recognized that effective planning requires long-term financial commitments. The instability of export proceeds works against long-range planning in that it is extremely hazardous to project future export proceeds. Obviously, if earnings are below expectations, a downward readjustment in developmental expenditures and forced restrictions of imports become mandatory. Even if there is a windfall increase—for example, unusually high export earnings of a transitory nature—the country may not be in the position to utilize this increment to the best advantage.

INDEBTEDNESS

When export income fails, there is a temptation to maintain imports and to offset the loss of foreign exchange through a heavier load of foreign debt. Occasionally, further indebtedness can be justified where the termination of projects already in process would entail losses not commensurate with long-run expectations. Where capital has already been sunk in a major project such as a dam, temporary suspension of construction would defer the benefit of the capital already invested, require the maintenance of that portion of the project already completed, and necessitate the costly reassembling of equipment and personnel at some future date. Even a slowdown in construction may not be economically justifiable.

However, much too frequently, high import levels are sustained for other reasons. The regime in power may seek to maintain popularity by a steady flow of consumer goods. Furthermore, governments feel compelled to project a dynamic image of progress and development. The population, understandably enough, has become aware of the benefits of development and expects its government to promote its welfare. Thus politicians placate the masses by such gambits as subsidizing bread and cloth and shore up the loyalty of the elites through the continued importation of luxury items. At another level, the military, which represents an important bulwark of governmental power, is favored by the purchase of sophisticated hardware. Even where the equipment is "free," its operating and maintenance costs can place an intolerable burden on the national budget.

Private and public interests in developed countries share complicity in the unnecessary increase in the indebtedness of underdeveloped countries. Governments in industrial countries guarantee payment for the sales to underdeveloped countries by domestic producers. This permits their industries to remain competitive and is an inexpensive way of supporting employment and output in sick industries. The recipient countries are only too willing to buy now and pay later, a situation analogous to the manner in which the poor in developed countries are attracted to installment buying. When the day of reckoning comes, few of the participants can be deemed blameless, as the recent investigations in Ghana clearly indicate.[13]

The magnitude of underdeveloped country indebtedness incurred to finance imports (supplier credits) has reached the phenomenal figure of about 4 billion dollars gross per year in the mid-1960's and now represents roughly a fourth of total indebtedness.[14] Total indebtedness in underdeveloped countries has been increasing rapidly since World War II. From 1950 onward, external public debt has grown at a rate of over a billion a year in the twenty-one underdeveloped countries studied by the International Bank for Reconstruction and Development. For thirty-seven countries sampled by the IBRD, public and publicly guaranteed debt rose from 7 billion to 18.2 billion dollars in the 1955–1962 period. As of December 31, 1965, total outstanding public debt for underdeveloped countries (including low-income Mediterranean countries) totalled 36.4 billion dollars.[15] Quite naturally, the debt service burden for underdeveloped countries has increased immensely. In 1958 debt service payments were approximately 7.5 percent of total external earnings; presently debt service amounts to about 10 percent. For the thirty-seven sample countries, debt interest payments increased from 700 million dollars in 1956 to 2.4 billion dollars in 1963. As of December 31, 1965, debt service and amortization payment totalled 3.5 billion dollars, including 0.4 billion for Southern Europe.[16]

Given this structure of debt and the yearly necessity to meet obligations either by payment or refinancing, the flow of external financial resources, private and public, barely offsets the balance of payments debt service and profit repatriation. Down to 1956, the

[13] *West Africa*, No. 2576 (October 15, 1966), "Firms and Bribes," pp. 1169–1170, and "A 'Clearing House' for Bribes," p. 1171.

[14] International Bank for Reconstruction and Development and the International Development Association, *1965–1966 Annual Report*, Washington, D.C., 1966, p. 35.

[15] Dragoslav Avramovic, *Economic Growth and External Growth*, Baltimore, 1965, pp. 4 and 107; and A. K. Cairncross, *Factors in Economic Development*, London, 1962, p. 56.

[16] Avramovic, *op. cit.*, pp. 4 and 107, and IBRD and IDA, *op. cit.*, p. 33.

underdeveloped countries as a whole had a favorable trade balance. The major contributors to this surplus were the oil-producing countries of the Middle East and Venezuela. From 1956 onward, the underdeveloped countries have been running import surpluses, with a number of exceptions, which include again the oil-producing countries. Fortunately for the underdeveloped countries, a large portion of this negative balance has been offset by grants from developed countries. In recent years, however, the developed countries have evidenced an increasing unwillingness to make outright gifts and have preferred instead to make other arrangements, such as long-term and low-interest loans.

THE PROBLEM OF PLANNING

The planning problems caused by international financial difficulties are generally compounded by the attitudes toward planning present in the countries themselves. Since World War II, it has become generally recognized that planning can be an effective instrument of economic advance. The observation of successful planning, or at least financial management, in economically advanced countries had led to plans being considered a positive attribute in themselves. In such a situation a plan takes on a life of its own, irrespective of its operational relationship to the economy; a plan, in short, is an attribute of sovereignty and a badge of modernization which no self-respecting underdeveloped country would be without. In Latin America the phenomenon of *proyectismo*, or project-consciousness, pervades governmental bureaucracies. There, economic problems are "resolved" by economic plans, much in the same spirit that political difficulties are "overcome" by writing constitutions and passing laws. This should not be taken simply as an indictment of Latin America, for these sentiments and attitudes are widely shared throughout much of the underdeveloped world. This ritual of planning is not without its participants from the developed world: eminent economists are called in to aid in the writing of the plan, and later others are asked to review and revise it periodically.

In order to organize human activity effectively for development, that is, planning, a vast amount of knowledge is needed in the form of accurate statistical data, which are seldom available. Nonquantifiable data are equally important and are seldom taken into consideration. Even such elementary statistics as gross population size cannot always be counted on. Recently we had the spectacle in Nigeria of a major political controversy over the acceptance of a census.

Most of the developed countries have a long tradition—in most cases, over one hundred years of experience—of collecting and analyzing statistical data about population and national resources. A body of techniques aimed at interpretation, eliminating error, and improving overall reliability have evolved as a concomitant of economic and industrial development. Some of these techniques are certainly transferable, but others are specific to the historical circumstances of the countries in which they evolved. Much important work is being done in borrowing, adapting, and developing techniques for use in developing countries. It is also true, though, that statisticians and other experts, who are used to the levels of confidence typical of developed nations, assume a nearly comparable situation in the underdeveloped world. The temptation to apply highly sophisticated statistical approaches is strong and finds an enthusiastic reception among the leaders of the underdeveloped world.[17]

The truth is that the condition of underdevelopment is applicable to both the economies of the lands in question and their presently available statistics. The statistical priorities in the underdeveloped world should be directed toward gathering basic statistics, such as data on agricultural production, school attendance, functional literacy, industrial output, skills, the composition of the labor force, and so forth. It is only on the basis of such a solid foundation that effective planning, not to mention long-term projections, can be structured.

PROJECT PLANNING AND FEASIBILITY STUDIES

Given the dearth of reliable statistical and general information, an interim substitute is available in the form of specific feasibility studies. In a previous chapter we referred to the abysmal failure of the Tanganyika Groundnut Scheme. There a feasibility study was conducted, but the inquiry assumed the presence of ecological and

[17] Ashok Mitra, "Underdeveloped Statistics," *Economic Development and Culture Change*, Vol. XI, No. 3, Pt. 1, 1963, pp. 315–317.

economic conditions totally contrary to the realities of Southern Tanganyika. More recently, the Northern Nigeria Development Corporation dispensed with feasibility studies in order not to delay the construction of a cement plant. After a cement plant was purchased from Germany, shipped across the Sahara, and erected on the chosen location, it was found that the quality of the local limestone precluded the production of cement.[18] While this is a dramatic and exceptional case, the lack of an adequate feasibility study may often lead to greater cost and lower quality of production than was anticipated.

A feasibility study requires a knowledge of the availability and quality of local resources, sources of supply of parts or other primary aspects of production, the pool of skilled or trainable labor, the carrying capacity of transportation both for supply and distribution, and the potential market for the product, either in the form of consumer demand or to meet the needs of secondary industries.

Obviously, feasibility studies vary as to the project intended, but for all large-scale enterprises a range of factors, not all of them obvious, must be taken into consideration. Thus, a hydroelectric, irrigation, or water control scheme must in part cope with purely technical factors: geology, soil, the regimen of the river, and so forth. No less important, though, may be an understanding of the economic and social patterns of the riverine people, a thorough evaluation of communication needs and, where applicable, planning for the utilization of generated power.

The Papaloapan River Project of Southern Mexico is an example of the opportunities, together with hazards, of complex developmental schemes. The project, started in 1947, aimed at accomplishing a variety of worthwhile objectives, chief among these being flood control, production of hydroelectric power, and the utilization through irrigation of otherwise marginal lands.

The Papaloapan basin covers portions of the states of Veracruz, Oaxaca, and Puebla and is located directly to the west of the Isthmus of Tehuantepec. The Papaloapan River and its tributaries empty into the Gulf of Mexico near its southernmost point. This is one of the least developed areas of Mexico and, with proper use, has the potential of relieving some of the population pressures of the central plateau and contributing to the food needs of the nation.

---

[18] The limestone was found to be too "wet" for the machinery purchased, and as a result the equipment will have to be replaced. *A White Paper on the Military Government Policy for the Re-organization of the Northern Nigeria Development Corporation*, Kaduna, 1966

For a variety of reasons it was decided to proceed with the project prior to the termination of feasibility studies. As in the case of the Nigerian cement scheme, this proved to be a most expensive short cut. While much has been accomplished, the project has been dogged with disappointment and waste. As Poleman's study of the project shows, an expensive highway was built through an area lacking all-weather feeder roads; a city for a population of 150,000, Ciudad Alemán, was laid out without considering the potentials of the already established nearby cities; inadequate attention was paid to the patterns of life and attitudes toward authority of some of the local inhabitants, in particular the Mazatec Indians; the demand for hydroelectric power was overestimated roughly by a factor of four; and the inadequacies of agricultural research led to the failure of a number of irrigation-based agricultural schemes. As the author observes, "One can only conclude that during its first six years the Papaloapan Project contained characteristics of the proverbial *proyectismo* of Latin America."[19]

Any enterprise of economic development requires information in order to be carried out effectively. Feasibility studies are a means of obtaining information about particular projects. But when these projects are considered in terms of national economic goals, other factors come into play, factors that may be masked when the frame of reference is limited to a particular project and its immediate economic impact.

PRIORITIES FOR COORDINATED DEVELOPMENT PLANNING

The overall objectives of national economic planning should determine to a substantial extent the order of priority of projects studied for feasibility but, in turn, the results of these studies influence, or at least should influence, the planning perspective. In a scheme of national planning, projects should be considered in relation to other projects in order to determine whether they are complementary or contradictory. Thus a particular project or series of projects may not be feasible in isolation, but when taken together

[19] Thomas T. Poleman, *The Papaloapan Project: Agricultural Development in the Mexican Tropics*, Stanford, Calif., 1964, p. 103. See also pp. 115, 119, 100.

in a coordinated plan, they may provide the missing element of viability. An industrial complex, for instance, may be uneconomical because of lack of transportation, and a transportation system under current conditions may be unwarranted because of lack of demand; but, in conjunction, they may be self-supporting and contribute to national economic development. Of course, any well-prepared enterprise is potentially viable. The problem is that there always exist limitations as to what a nation can accomplish in any given planning period, and this is why it is necessary to establish priorities in terms of overall contribution to economic development.

A coordinated plan for development must consider the pool of educated and trained talent available. Too often it is assumed that, if a nation has sufficient financial resources to budget a development plan, it will automatically come into being. Even after the planner has established a list of priorities aimed at further national development, there are still the competing manpower demands generated by the process of development. Often, while at one level the projects of a plan may be complementary in that they provide mutually reinforcing goods and services, at another level they are competitive in that they are vying for the same human resources.

Another covert hazard of national plans for development is the frequent failure of governments and agencies to recognize that projects, once in being, require a constant flow of skills and funds to keep them operating at their optimum level. Many of the most vital aspects of a development plan are not self-financing, or are self-financing only in the long-term. Virtually every underdeveloped country recognizes the critical importance of education and allocates a sizeable portion of its budget to this end. In many instances, though, education is considered primarily in terms of school construction and the number of new classrooms built yearly, tangibles that are often used as an index of educational achievement. Not only does an expansion in schools call for funds to pay and train teachers, a factor widely recognized, but there is also the requirement for the maintenance of physical facilities.

The deteriorated conditions of many recently built schools in a number of underdeveloped countries (Mexico, for example) indicate a lack of appreciation of the necessity for upkeep. Both in rural and urban areas the visitor to Mexico soon fails to be surprised at school buildings, sometimes of definite esthetic quality and good construction, marred by boarded windows and peeling walls.

Many countries distinguish between an operating and a development budget. The cost of building a project is borne by the development budget, while the maintenance cost tends to be shifted to the operating budget. Projects in planning may add to the burden of the operating budget in the future and place a strain on funds and resources destined for development at that time. Phrased differently, there is a direct relationship between projects completed and budgetary demands. There are costs that can be expected to rise as the factors of time and wear come increasingly into play. The full cost of a project must be considered and development planning adjusted not only to present needs but also to future expectations. Worthwhile projects with long-term costs can be justified if the funds and staff allocated to them contribute to a meaningful rise in future levels of national income and national competence.

PLANNING FOR TECHNOLOGICAL LEADERSHIP

Some developmental activities cannot be judged solely in terms of a limited cost-effectiveness type of analysis. There are definite and definable advantages, though these may be delayed for a long period, in having leading sectors in science and technology. The condition of underdevelopment does not preclude excellence in some areas of progress. Leadership in these areas takes years of accrued experience, and continued economic development in the future would be stunted unless provision is made in the present for the training of scientific and technological elites. Consequently, projects must be judged not only on the basis of their direct economic contribution but also on what can best be described as their educational value.

As we have shown elsewhere, the acquaintanceship with modern science and technology provides both a stimulus for reevaluating traditional outlook and a basis for modernization. The value of allocating resources to highly sophisticated scientific and technological endeavors is demonstrated by India's advanced development in the field of atomic energy and Mexico's leading position in the field of heart research. In India, which is critically short of fuels, the development of atomic energy is a first-order priority. Most of the research in this area can and is being done in developed countries. However, the adaptation of this knowledge to meet India's needs requies the existence of a local cadre of trained personnel and the experience in developing and using the necessary complex equipment.

Already India has an established atomic energy foundation, which puts her in the position of utilizing, even perhaps pioneering, new technical breakthroughs congruent with her diversified economic needs.[20] Mexico's position in heart research has attracted students and medical practitioners from abroad and has contributed to the improvement of the general quality of medicine in the Republic.

With the help of international agencies, many underdeveloped countries are assuming a leading role in agricultural research. While a certain risk exists that the expected breakthroughs will not materialize, when and if they do, they make a contribution to one of the most vital needs of underdeveloped countries: agricultural progress. Recent discoveries in rice cultivation in the Philippines offer the promise of raising the standard of living of millions of people. Even a small agricultural improvement, if it can be widely diffused, may benefit vast numbers of cultivators.

One great advantage of locally derived improvements, both in agriculture and in other areas, is that they are more likely to be geared to meet the needs of the local economy and fit the cultural and environmental patterns of the area. These innovations are locally available, and the personnel associated with their development probably have some contact with those who are the intended beneficiaries of this research. The problem of transmission may therefore be greatly facilitated.

CONCLUSIONS

Although the prognosis for some underdeveloped countries appears good, in general we can expect the problems facing these countries today to continue into the future. While this is a distressing projection, it is one that seems to fit reality as we see it. In many regions the resources for the tasks of transformation do not begin to match the magnitude of the problem. Even as we write, India's main preoccupation is less that of advancing a standard of living than providing foodstuffs to keep the bulk of the population from starvation. True, the subcontinent has experienced a sequence of bad agricultural years, but given the present conditions of agricultural

[20] H. J. Bhabha, "Science and the Problems of Development," *Science*, Vol. 151, No. 3710, February 4, 1966, pp. 541–548.

practice and population growth, even "normal" levels of production fall below the generally recognized standards of nutritional needs. India has been saved from disaster by the aid and bounty of the developed countries at a level that cannot be continued indefinitely. American surplus grain stocks, which have been of pivotal importance during the past few years, are now virtually exhausted. No comparable stocks exist elsewhere and, of course, the world shortage of food is on the increase.

Undoubtedly India poses the most severe problems of agricultural development and institutional change. Nevertheless, similar problems are to be encountered throughout the underdeveloped world. Furthermore, in many nations economic development has tended to become a preoccupation secondary to the elementary problem of maintaining national integrity and internal stability. Political and ideological conflict, factional strife, linguistic and religious rivalries, tribal animosities, are all antithetical to progressive development. Quite apart from the disruption that these engender, underdeveloped countries can count on only a small number of skilled and educated personnel whose energies should properly be directed to questions of development. Also, such an environment is hardly conducive to attracting foreign technical assistance.

In many cases understandable patriotic sentiments have forced the adoption of a local language as the official medium of instruction and communication. This adds a burden in that it tends to isolate the country from the mainstream of international scientific and technological development and may in some instances exacerbate minority antagonism or lead to a proliferation of official languages. Some of these internal political difficulties are not without their counterparts in developed countries. Certainly cultural and religious rivalries are a source of conflict in such countries as Canada, Belgium, and the Balkans. In the United States it is frequently necessary to give a religious and ethnic balance to a political ticket, and the necessity is often felt to distribute Federal favors on a regional basis. The underlying particularisms, while frequently intense, do not lead to mass bloodshed and cataclysmic breakdowns in the national structure. A good theoretical argument could be presented that the process of selecting individuals on ethnic, religious, or regional basis retards development; yet the pool of talent in developed countries is large enough so that any retardation occurring is almost imperceptible.

Whatever the magnitude of the problems of the underdeveloped countries, and however dismal the future may appear, the affluent are not in a position to dismiss the issue. The world we live in today has become increasingly interrelated, and what affects one will in some way or another, sooner or later, affect all. If anything, the gap between the rich and the poor has increased, while the acceptibility of this gap has decreased. In our modern world the condition of poverty is not easily tolerated, as witnessed, for instance, by the discontent of the underprivileged within the United States, particularly the Negro people. Both at home and abroad there is a recognition that these problems should be tackled. Rather than disengage themselves, the developed countries have become increasingly involved in the political and economic affairs of the third world. Much of this involvement is economically questionable in that it tends to center on questions of ideology and military confrontation. What is called for is a major coordinated effort on the part of both the developed and the underdeveloped countries, an effort that transcends the prejudices and sensitivities of all participants. There must be a willingness to learn, just as there must be a commitment to tutor, not to indoctrinate. Problems must be approached pragmatically with a willingness to adjust and compromise. The magnitude of the problem demands a massive effort, financial and technical, far surpassing anything that has been done to date. Whatever the price, one can predict that the cost, both human and financial, of ignoring these problems is bound to be greater.

It is currently being questioned in the United States whether the country can afford both "butter" at home and "guns" in Vietnam. One may question the economic feasibility of high government expenditures for internal programs and external military involvements; what is clear is that present levels of military expenditure (over 20 billion dollars per annum on Vietnam alone) cut sharply into potential aid funds. Modern war dissipates substance at an entirely unprecedented level.

Bibliography

Agarwala, A. N. and S. P. Singh (eds.), *The Economics of Underdevelopment*, Bombay, 1958.

Ayres, C. E., *Theory of Economic Progress*, New York, 1962.

Balogh, Thomas, *The Economics of Poverty*, London, 1965.

Balogh, Thomas, *Unequal Partners*, London, 1965.

Baran, Paul, *The Political Economy of Growth*, New York, 1957.

Bauer, P. T., *West African Trade*, London, 1954.

Birmingham, W., I. Neustadt, and E. N. Omaboe (eds.), *A Study of Contemporary Ghana*, Vols. I & II, London, 1966, 1967.

Cairncross, A. K., *Factors in Economic Development*, London, 1962.

Furtado, Celso, *The Economic Growth of Brazil*, Berkeley and Los Angeles, 1963.

Gordon, Wendell, *The Political Economy of Latin America*, New York, 1966.

Herskovits, M. J. and M. Harwitz (eds.), *Economic Transition in Africa*, Evanston, Ill., 1964.

Hirschman, A. O. (ed), *Latin American Issues*, New York, 1961.

Hirschman, A. O., *The Strategy of Economic Development*, New Haven, Conn., 1958.

Horowitz, I. L., *Three Worlds of Development*, New York, 1966.

Leibenstein, Harvey, *Economic Backwardness and Economic Growth*, 1963.

Lewis, W. Arthur, *Development Planning*, New York, 1966.

Meier, Richard L., *Development Planning*, New York, 1965.

Myint, Hla, *The Economics of the Developing Countries*, New York, 1965.

Nurkse, Ragnar, *Problems of Capital Formation in Underdeveloped Countries*, Oxford, 1953.

Pepelasis, A., L. Mears, and I. Adleman (eds.), *Economic Development*, New York, 1961.

Schatz, Sayre P., *Development Bank Lending in Nigeria*, Ibadan, 1964.

Author Index

Subject Index

133